The Films of
WARREN BEATTY

The Films of

WARREN BEATTY

by

Lawrence J. Quirk

THE CITADEL PRESS · Secaucus, New Jersey

For Michael Ritzer and Arthur Tower, two good and proven friends.

First edition
Copyright © 1979 by Lawrence J. Quirk
All rights reserved
Published by Citadel Press
A division of Lyle Stuart Inc.
120 Enterprise Ave., Secaucus, N.J. 07094
In Canada: George J. McLeod Limited
Don Mills, Ontario
Designed by Dennis J. Grastorf
Manufactured in the United States of America

Library of Congress Cataloging in Publication Data

Quirk, Lawrence J
  The films of Warren Beatty.

  1. Beatty, Warren, 1937-   2. Moving-picture
actors and actresses — United States — Biography.
I. Title.
PN2287.B394Q5   791.43'028'0924 [B]   79-480
ISBN 0-8065-0670-9

Acknowledgments

Mark Ricci and *The Memory Shop,* New York; Ernest D. Burns and *Cinemabilia,* New York; Paul Myers and the staff of the New York Public Library's Theatre and Film Collection, Library & Museum of Performing Arts, New York, and Mr. Myers' assistants: Rod Bladel, Maxwell Silverman, Dorothy Swerdlove, Betty Wharton, Donald Fowle, Monty Arnold and David Bartholomew; Metro-Goldwyn-Mayer, Warner Bros., Columbia, 20th Century-Fox.

And James E. Runyan, Michael Ritzer, John Cocchi, John A. Guzman, Doug McClelland, Don Koll.

Contents

Warren Beatty: Actor and Man

WARREN BEATTY has always been an actor who doesn't like to act. He has made only fifteen movies in seventeen years. He has detoured on several occasions to produce the films in which he has starred (*Bonnie and Clyde*, 1967; *Shampoo*, 1975), and produced *and* directed his 1978 release, *Heaven Can Wait*. Politics and women have taken up as much of his attention over the years as has his acting career. He lives his own life his own way, and at forty-one (as of March 30, 1978) he has never married. But he is canny about money, and has made many millions from his carefully arranged percentage deals. In his teens he told a high school sweetheart, now Mrs. Ann Colgan of Ardsley, New York, that "the only reason he would marry would be to have a child— and that would be to satisfy his ego." And when sister Shirley MacLaine told an interviewer, "Warren's very much into money," his comeback was: "In our system there's nothing foolish about money, so when you have made a lot of money they take you seriously."

Beatty has never troubled himself unduly about being liked or disliked, and has been termed: "A very private man who only incidentally toils in a very public business." He has had perhaps as busy a sex life as any man in films, and with a wide variety of female partners, some of them well-publicized dalliances, but resolutely refuses to discuss this aspect of his life. "Not only is it bad taste, but there are others involved, so I would be betraying their privacy as well as my

own," he answers when pressed on more personal matters.

George Stevens, who directed Beatty in *The*

Only Game in Town (1970), once described him as "like an iceberg, in the sense that what you see of him on the surface is no part of him at all. He is not lighthearted and frivolous. He is scholarly, headstrong, stubborn and tough." Shirley Mac-Laine compared their natures thus: "Warren sees things in terms of black and white. I see the gray, the nuance. I tend to be more philosophical and abstract." But Sister Shirley is not without humor re Warren. Asked once what she thought about Beatty's abortive plan to film a porno extravaganza, she said, "I'll ask him if I can co-star; I haven't seen him in the nude since he was six, and I'd sure as hell like to find out what all the shouting is about!"

Beatty has spent his recent years ensconced in a large suite at the Beverly Wilshire Hotel, which a friend has called "abnormally cluttered and frenetic, as any busy man's pad should be." Asked by an interviewer why he preferred hotel living, he said, "For one thing I can come and go whenever I like, and that's important because I spend a lot of time elsewhere." ("Elsewhere" is rumored to be not only a large house he owns nearby, but also the homes of various lady-loves.) Refusing to be lured into "sex talk," he said of all that had been written and rumored of his sex life: "If I tried to keep up with what was said of me sexually, I would be, as Sinatra once said, speaking to you from a jar in the University of Chicago Medical Center."

There is a wide variety of opinion on Warren Beatty. He has been called "kind and sensitive, a true gentleman, courtly to ladies, considerate of his friends." And he has also been called "more boy than man, yes even at forty-one; confused, venal, money-mad, satyriacal, insensitive to others, opportunistic and self-absorbed."

Like the late James Dean, Beatty established his cinematic legend in his three earliest films, and many consider these three his best. While he shuffled, shambled and squinted in the best Dean manner, and while his voice had many of the tricks and inflections of Marlon Brando, with a few Monty Clift shadings thrown in for good measure, the screen persona that burst upon the nation in 1961 ("pensive-browed, sensual-lipped," as one critic described it at the time) was very much Warren Beatty's own.

In *Splendor in the Grass,* his first film, he played a virile, sturdy, well-intentioned young man buffeted, and in time overwhelmed, by the oppressive Puritan conventions of a 1928 small-town Kansas ambience. He was effective among other reasons because he was obviously identifying with the stultifying, soul-killing conditions of his own Virginia youth. In *The Roman Spring of Mrs. Stone,* his second 1961 film, he gave a performance considered by many Beatty aficionados his all-time best, as a cynical Italian gigolo whose psyche has been distorted by harrowing WW II experiences, and who preys cynically on rich older women. For Beatty this role represented a total escape psychically to an exotic continental milieu, an acting-out of the erotic, even sadistic, fantasies of his repressed and conformist childhood and adolescence. In *All Fall Down* (1962), his third picture, Beatty was again playing one of the extensions of his secret self—a confused, guilt-ridden young man, bedevilled by incompatible parents, whose hunger for women goes hand in hand with a misogynistic refusal to accept permanent commitment, the Boy-Man Transcendent. In all three films Beatty was extremely effective, and they made him a major star by age twenty-five.

Then, because he didn't really enjoy acting and had become confused and alienated by all the hoopla of fame, Beatty took a two-year sabbatical, after which he made some wrong artistic choices—*Lilith, Mickey One*—with the best and most sincere intentions. For a change of pace he then tried light comedy, but floundered in the insubstantial *Promise Her Anything.* He then got himself into some awkward cavortings in a meretricious, hollow-spirited "caper" film, *Kaleidoscope—then,* battered, bloody but unbowed, hitched up his pants, squared his jaw and plunged at long last into the cynical big-money rat-race that he had hitherto scorned, and parlayed, as producer and star, the violent and jazzy *Bonnie and Clyde* into one of the most controversial and financially profitable hits Hollywood had ever known. After another long sabbatical, during which he traveled, romanced the women, and dabbled in politics, he got burned trying to do a quiet, contained, sensitively depicted George Stevens love story, *The Only Game in Town,* with Elizabeth Taylor, which did abysmal box-office business. From then on Beatty went for what he considered "sure things"—a whorehouse owner in the Old West, a bank robbery "caper," assassina-

Warren Beatty and Joan Fontaine in "The Visitor" (one of the One Step Beyond *TV series, 1959).*

17

Meditating on the set of Mickey One

Greeting fans at a Beverly Hills party

tion intrigue, a satyr hairdresser in 1968 Hollywood, another caper — a kidnapping — with 1930s nostalgia-frosting.

Many feel that if Beatty had stayed on the track of his first three film performances and had held out for roles that expressed true, honest and legitimate aspects of his private mystique and highly-individualized dream-scheme, he might have gone on to a truly prestigious and highly respected career within a limited framework of audience addressal. Instead, he surrendered to the blandishments of the Bitch Goddess Success, and proceeded to get himself spectacularly miscast in a variety of roles beyond his interpretive range while selecting tasteless, gory and sexy movies because his instinct told them that they would be box-office winners. "Art and Commerce fought a battle within him and Commerce won," as an associate has put it. Add to this some shrewd publicity and promotional bulldozing of press and public, and you have the formula for Beatty Success: 1970s style.

Beatty has loved, and been loved by, a number of famous actresses — Joan Collins, Natalie Wood, Leslie Caron, Julie Christie among others, not to mention lesser lights and assorted unknowns — and has managed to remain friends with all of them once the dew went off the rose and he felt constrained to move on. He is accused of being bull-headed and arrogant and insensitive and spoiled and power-mad, yet he is on occasion capable of surprising humility and self-insights.

"I'm not an actor," he insists. "I'm a person who sometimes acts. An *actor* acts, he continues to act, and as often as not, he acts in the theatre. He needs to act. He needs to go into different characters, to explore them and to play them, to get out of one person's reality and into another person's reality. So I'm not a good person to talk to about that. I respect acting, though, but it frightens me a little bit, and it bores me a little bit sometimes. *I'm* more of a person, I feel. I don't really know what I am. I sort of make films once in a while. If I have a subject I want to say something about, I will play a character on that subject, but I need to play that character because I get to know that character very well, and then I want to say something."

To another interviewer Beatty confessed: "I'm a rather self-indulgent, lazy, sort of fun-seeking person who's been very lucky through the years to be as affluent as I've been and to have the choices that I've had. In many ways you have to count points against me for seriousness about film. I think it's better to be straightforward about that. Let's just leave it that when it comes to acting in the films, once in a while I feel I have something to say and say it."

Beatty also manifests a certain laissez-faire-style humility when asked to explain such films as *Shampoo.* "It's silly to attack someone's perception of a symbol that they see in a film, because who are you to say that that's not it? Who am I to say that the film is not something that you say it is? You may know more about this film than I do . . ."

Asked why he chooses certain film subjects and how he approaches them, the sometime-producer-regularly-actor stumbles inarticulately and replies: "At a certain point you just say, 'Well, I'll trust what I'm doing; it's got to be what I *must* be doing.' I guess I'm saying what I mean."

When another reporter read him an early review that stated: "[Beatty's] acting style is somewhat rusty and rudimentary; stares and long silences and fumblings and flounderings are conspicuous in his limited bag of tricks; he has no technique to fall back on, and sex chemistry alone has put him over—he looks sexy, he talks sexy, he acts sexy and this gets several million feminine hormones jumping cross-country and so he is a star, even though usually an absentee one"—Beatty chuckled and conceded that there was a certain amount of truth in the statement. He reacted the same way to another notice that harped on his "broad-shouldered, slack-mouthed, sensual-lipped, bedroom-eyed sexy squinting" as the secret of his stellar appeal. About his acting he would only say, "I'm not Method or anything like that; I just—hell, I just do it!"

After first telling a reporter that he was, and is, against the idea of film as propaganda, he added, "But on the other hand, you can't run away from it. One could attack *Shampoo,* for instance, propagandistically. My God, you certainly could—the feminist movement could attack it, the serious forward-seeking optimist in American politics could attack it, capitalists, communists, everybody could attack it—because it doesn't seem to put any of its characters in a very admirable, positive light. But I think what has happened is that American filmmakers of the mid-1970s have drawn negative conclusions from their basic perceptions, and that's what the films are about."

He is frankly doubtful about what he calls "inspirational films." "Sometimes, to show a struggle can be inspiring . . . A story demands conflict for it to be a story, and for it to be a great

With Jane Fonda

Beatty relaxes with a newspaper on a film set.

story, there has to be some great conflict. And this conflict in a large struggle is going to be assumed to be negative, and to overcome obstacles successfully, I suppose, is an inspiration." And while he is willing to concede that the more romantic films of the 1920s to the 1940s, the stories that stressed triumph over adversity of all kinds, were of the kind that "gave hope," they were, in his view, "unrealistic."

Katharine Hepburn in 1975 publicly castigated Beatty for not using his money, power and prestige to make affirmative, positive films that stressed the eternal verities like love and idealism. Certainly the Beatty film work of the 1970s reflects a negative, cynical, opportunistic attitude. "I think he tried other approaches and was disillusioned—art films, capers, what-not. He now subscribes to the theory that the success of any business is measured by its profits. Yes, that Success principle, playing to what he conceives to be mass desires and needs, guides him now." This from a long-time associate.

Nor is he thrown off by reporters articulating to him such ironies of his career as the fact that he has maintained a macho, unimpeachably heterosexual stance though he owed his original stardom to homosexual artists whose works gave him an expressive persona. "It takes all kinds. I respect artists no matter what color coat they wear," he has said. "To live at all is to understand the human condition. Where you live it, how you live it, in what style you live it—that isn't the point; the point is that to live is to experience the human condition as totally as your neighbor. And if you and he like different flavors of ice cream in some areas, so what?"

It all began for Warren Beatty in Richmond, Virginia, on March 30, 1937. He was the son of Ira O. Beaty (he added the extra "t" later when he became an actor) and the former Kathlyn MacLean. Ira Beaty, who formerly was a high school principal, later became a realtor. He was from all reports a cold, stuffy, conformist man, strict with discipline, outer-directed, rigid. His mother was more imaginative, indeed romantic and poetic by temperament, but from all reports she deferred to his father in all things and abandoned her dreams to settle into the small-town conventional mold. His mother had an interest in amateur dramatics and encouraged him along those lines. His father, a stickler for education, reportedly taught

Answering questions from the press in 1961 at the time of his first starring picture

He closes his eyes and says nothing when another interviewer asks him a personal question.

Greeting his audience during one of his rare public speeches

him to read at the age of five. There was an older sister, three years his senior, who left home in her late teens to go into show business. She revamped her mother's maiden name and became Shirley MacLaine.

Beatty has always refused to discuss his early life in detail and at one point asked his parents to refuse all interviews on the subject. He seems to have had a lonely and unhappy childhood and adolescence and once admitted, "I felt different from the other kids — I didn't just know how I was, but I knew I was."

At Washington and Lee High School in Arlington, Virginia, where the Beatys had moved when Warren was quite small, he paid his conformist dues by joining the football team, where he became a star center. Earlier, he told an interviewer, "My childhood ambition was to be president of the United States. That was until I was six years old. At seven I decided to be governor of Georgia. At eight I decided to become an actor. People become actors because of a need within themselves. I got most of my acting ambitions temporarily pounded out of me in high school football." Later he was to say, "I never really decided to become an actor, just drifted along."

When he graduated from high school he received, he recalls, ten offers of football scholarships, but he rejected them. Once he told Hedda Hopper: "I developed into a fair player for a period of about a year, but I never could have been as successful in college football as they seemed to think I would. I didn't enjoy it that much. The important thing is doing what you enjoy, not because you get a reaction from others." He told another interviewer: "Pro football players work hard — damned hard. And there is always the danger of getting your teeth knocked out and your nose mashed in and your appearance spoiled beyond recall. I found that prospect unappetizing." Meanwhile, encouraged by the frustrated, introverted mother who had abandoned her own early dreams, and in typical "displacement-style" was attempting to live them out through him, he took

During a coffee break on the set of Mickey One, *1965*

With Elia Kazan during the making of Splendor in the Grass, *Summer 1960*

Director Kazan explains some of the fine points of his Bud Stamper characterization to Beatty during Splendor in the Grass *shooting, 1960.*

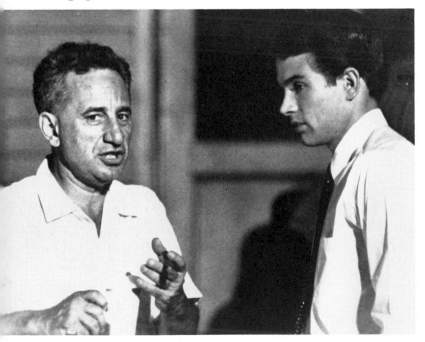

part extensively in the amateur theatricals which in time became his consuming interest.

Shirley MacLaine, who preceded Beatty as a star by some five years and who was to become a famous personality in her own right for roles in *The Apartment, Two for the Seesaw, The Children's Hour* and *Irma La Douce,* proved as voluble as her brother was reticent when dealing with their early life in Arlington, Virginia, and proceeded to let all the cats out of the bag in her autobiography, writing:

"Conformity was the rule of behavior in our neighborhood. We were all Baptists. Every single last modest tree-lined person on the block was a white Southern American middle-class Baptist. Oh, maybe there were a few Methodists but not enough to hurt. We lived according to what our neighbors thought and I guess they were living according to what *we* thought (which was wishing they would stop thinking what we were thinking)."

She added: "Because of Dad's somewhat distorted discipline and Mother's insistence that 'we were lucky to have such a lovely life, really' and the neighbors' twisted frustrations which permeated even the good times, Warren and I breathed the air of rebellion into each other. A kind of conniving rebellion to beat the system. It wasn't easy because the principal of the school we attended was our father, so we were expected to set a good example. How could we set a good example and still enjoy life? It took teamwork. Together we shared the responsibility of being model children. Warren never tracked mud into the house or ate cookies in the living room."

Miss MacLaine went on to say that outside the home they "really lived," emptying garbage pails on other people's front porches, punching holes in tires, setting off fire alarms, ringing doorbells. "All this was unknown to the stern figure who presided at the head of the dinner table. At the end of the day we would sit nodding agreement as he complained earnestly that delinquent kids were ruining the neighborhood. At the other end of the table Mother listened with a sad sparkle in her eyes, saying nothing."

MacLaine also remembers that against the background of familial pressure and stress personified by a stern and unimaginative father given to rigid conformist patterns and a sensitive, poetic-spirited mother who had retreated largely

Theatre, this time as an usher of sorts, then enrolled at Northwestern University's School of Speech and Drama. He gave up on this after a year and moved on to New York, where he became one of Stella Adler's students. Of Adler he said later, "She equipped me with a certain amount of arrogance—arrogant self-confidence, I should say—which enabled me to bluff my way through a few sidescrapers."

Finding it difficult to make ends meet, he lived in a furnished room on West 68th Street, weathered a long and discouraging siege of hepatitis, then got a part-time job playing the piano in a West 58th Street bar. He later took jobs as a sandhog on the new third tube of the Lincoln Tunnel and worked as a bricklayer's helper.

Finally came small breaks on TV ("Studio One," "Playhouse 90," and then the lead in Kraft Theatre's *The Curly Haired Kid.* Summer stock alternated with TV, and he played winters at the North Jersey Playhouse in Fort Lee, N.J. Among

ity Music Hall for the opening of Kalci-
66

At a 1971 press interview (with Gert Frobe)

into her truncated dreams, "[Warren] would skip football practice and sit down at the piano (an instrument he had early mastered) to beat the hell out of it. He used to work everything out on the piano. I didn't know then (because he was as shy about his inside self as all of us) that every afternoon while Mom and Dad were grocery shopping and I was at dancing class, Warren was in the basement acting out his soul to every Al Jolson record ever made and memorizing in detail every play Eugene O'Neill ever wrote."

MacLaine added: "I don't think either of us ever seriously considered that we wouldn't be able to make something of ourselves. We *had* to: it was the only way we'd have any respect for ourselves. We wanted to live up to whatever our potentials might be. The frustrating spectacle of people who hadn't, who had been afraid to, and were bitterly disappointed in themselves as a result, had been crippling to us in many ways as we grew up, but on the other hand, their failures and frustrations had been so clear that Warren and I had a precise blueprint of how *not* to be!"

And so the brother and sister learned to conduct themselves according to what they conceived was best for them as individuals, to scorn living by the opinions, smiles, frowns of others, for in the final analysis they could and should answer only to themselves. It was *themselves* they didn't want to disappoint, it was *themselves* they wanted to be proud of.

MacLaine nailed her and Warren's parents and their environment as "cliché-loving, middle-class." And she dwelt on "the stultifying pressure to conform." That "pressure to conform," that bred steel-like resistance in time to the trite, the banal, the constrictive, the mediocre, the regular and predictable, was to give the artist in Warren Beatty the poignancy and pointedness of expression that characterized his sterling performances in his first three films. And in that background may lie the reasons why to the age of forty-two he has never married.

In the summer of 1954, while still in high school, he was hired as a "rat watcher" at Washington's National Theatre. "I was supposed to stand in the alley and keep the rats from going in the stage door, but the only rats I ever got to see were those on the stage," he said later. After graduating from high school in 1955, age eighteen, he again was employed by the National

Conferring with director Robert Rossen and Jean Seberg on the set of Lilith, *1964*

At a New York fashion show demonstrating the "Kaleidoscope look," High Mod styles designed by Carnaby Street team of Marion Foale and Sally Tuffin

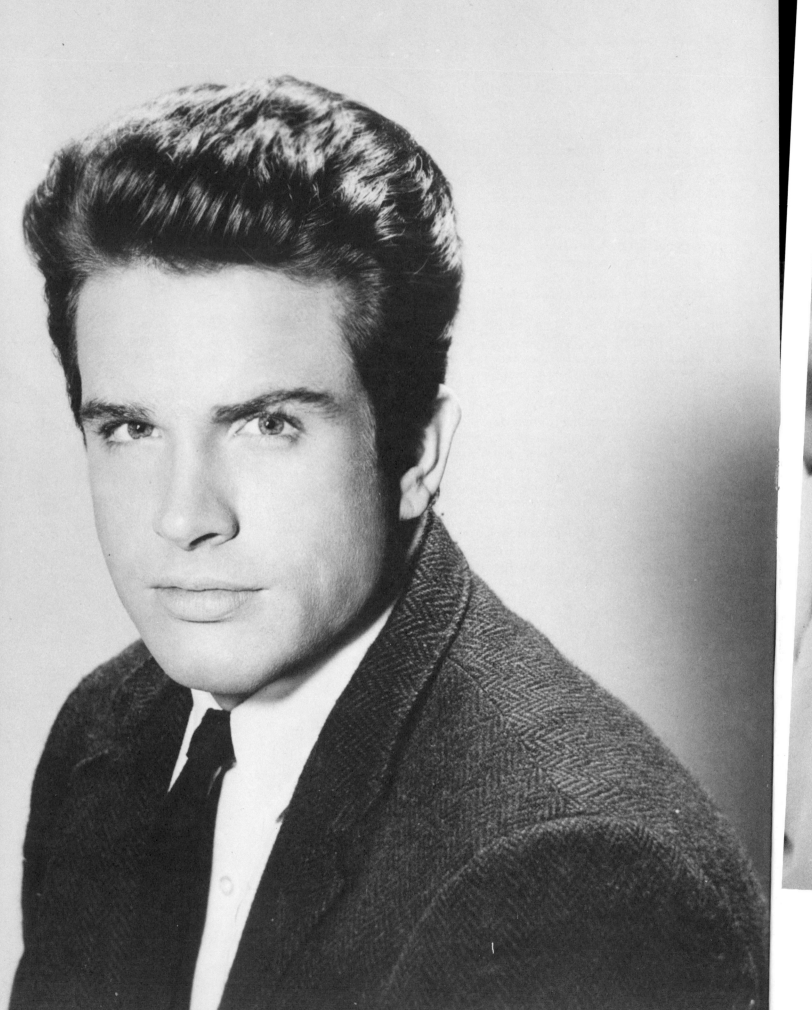

At Radio C
doscope, 19

33

into her truncated dreams, "[Warren] would skip football practice and sit down at the piano (an instrument he had early mastered) to beat the hell out of it. He used to work everything out on the piano. I didn't know then (because he was as shy about his inside self as all of us) that every afternoon while Mom and Dad were grocery shopping and I was at dancing class, Warren was in the basement acting out his soul to every Al Jolson record ever made and memorizing in detail every play Eugene O'Neill ever wrote."

MacLaine added: "I don't think either of us ever seriously considered that we wouldn't be able to make something of ourselves. We *had* to: it was the only way we'd have any respect for ourselves. We wanted to live up to whatever our potentials might be. The frustrating spectacle of people who hadn't, who had been afraid to, and were bitterly disappointed in themselves as a result, had been crippling to us in many ways as we grew up, but on the other hand, their failures and frustrations had been so clear that Warren and I had a precise blueprint of how *not* to be!"

And so the brother and sister learned to conduct themselves according to what they conceived was best for them as individuals, to scorn living by the opinions, smiles, frowns of others, for in the final analysis they could and should answer only to themselves. It was *themselves* they didn't want to disappoint, it was *themselves* they wanted to be proud of.

MacLaine nailed her and Warren's parents and their environment as "cliché-loving, middle-class." And she dwelt on "the stultifying pressure to conform." That "pressure to conform," that bred steel-like resistance in time to the trite, the banal, the constrictive, the mediocre, the regular and predictable, was to give the artist in Warren Beatty the poignancy and pointedness of expression that characterized his sterling performances in his first three films. And in that background may lie the reasons why to the age of forty-two he has never married.

In the summer of 1954, while still in high school, he was hired as a "rat watcher" at Washington's National Theatre. "I was supposed to stand in the alley and keep the rats from going in the stage door, but the only rats I ever got to see were those on the stage," he said later. After graduating from high school in 1955, age eighteen, he again was employed by the National

Conferring with director Robert Rossen and Jean Seberg on the set of Lilith, *1964*

At a New York fashion show demonstrating the "Kaleidoscope look," High Mod styles designed by Carnaby Street team of Marion Foale and Sally Tuffin

At Radio City Music Hall for the opening of Kalei-doscope, *1966*

Theatre, this time as an usher of sorts, then enrolled at Northwestern University's School of Speech and Drama. He gave up on this after a year and moved on to New York, where he became one of Stella Adler's students. Of Adler he said later, "She equipped me with a certain amount of arrogance—arrogant self-confidence, I should say—which enabled me to bluff my way through a few sidescrapers."

Finding it difficult to make ends meet, he lived in a furnished room on West 68th Street, weathered a long and discouraging siege of hepatitis, then got a part-time job playing the piano in a West 58th Street bar. He later took jobs as a sandhog on the new third tube of the Lincoln Tunnel and worked as a bricklayer's helper.

Finally came small breaks on TV ("Studio One," "Playhouse 90," and then the lead in Kraft Theatre's *The Curly Haired Kid*. Summer stock alternated with TV, and he played winters at the North Jersey Playhouse in Fort Lee, N.J. Among

At a 1971 press interview (with Gert Frobe)

Informal fun combined with rehearsing with Alexandra Stewart on the set of Mickey One, *Chicago, 1965 (Chicago lake skyline in rear)*

the plays he did in stock were *Visit to a Small Planet, The Happiest Millionaire, A Hatful of Rain* and *Compulsion.*

While playing *Compulsion* at the North Jersey Playhouse, Beatty came to the attention of Joshua Logan, the director, and William Inge, the playwright, who witnessed his performance. Both were enthusiastic about his promise. He was then twenty-two. Logan arranged a screen test and Inge decided to write a play specially tailored to Beatty's talents, but first they cast him in Inge's new play, *A Loss of Roses* (1959) — later made (1962) into a film with Richard Beymer and Joanne Woodward — about an innocent small-town youngster who falls in love with a sophisti-

cated but heart-torn female entertainer. The play was directed by Daniel Mann, and had its initial tryout at the same National Theatre in Washington where Beatty had once rat-watched.

Some have speculated since that floodtide year 1959 as to Shirley MacLaine's role in her brother's first big break. Four years after her own start in films, she had become a big star, and though much publicity has been given out over the years about how Beatty refused to trade on his relationship with her and "did everything on his own," there is ground for suspicion that she brought her struggling brother to the attention of people in a position to help him. The MacLaine–Beatty relationship was said to have been cool and distant

for years, but MacLaine has tended to attribute this to career separations and maintains that the relationship between them, while fraught with occasional small misunderstandings, has remained consistently cordial.

However this may be, when *A Loss of Roses,* starring Betty Field, opened at the Eugene O'Neill Theatre in New York on November 29, 1959, it met with a frosty reception from the reviewers. Beatty, however, came through extremely well. Typical of the reviews were those of Kenneth Tynan ("Mr. Beatty, sensual around the lips and pensive around the brow, is excellent as the boy") and Walter Kerr ("Mr. Beatty's performance is mercurial, sensitive, excellent"). Carol Haney as the carnival entertainer and Betty Field as the mother were also praised.

A Loss of Roses closed after twenty-five per-formances, however. Beatty meanwhile had been deluged with offers, and later signed a nonexclusive contract with Metro-Goldwyn-Mayer.

As in *A Loss of Roses,* the action of his first film, *Splendor in the Grass,* took place in the Kansas of the 1920s. Inge and director Elia Kazan had finally readied Inge's original screenplay for the movie, and within months of *Roses'* termination, Beatty was playing in it, in New York locations. It was not released for another year, and by that time he had completed his work in *The Roman Spring of Mrs. Stone.* His reviews for his first film were excellent: "A new and major movie star, combining the little-boy-lost charms of the late James Dean, and the smouldering good looks of Marlon Brando" (*Life*); "Ten years of intensive work put in by a notable talent could not improve upon this particular characterization. Even if he

A deep discussion with co-star Julie Christie and director Robert Altman on the set of McCabe & Mrs. Miller, *1971*

*A quiet between-scenes moment with buddy and
co-star Jack Nicholson on the set of* The Fortune,
1975

With sister Shirley MacLaine and Pete Hamill

With Shirley MacLaine

With Shirley MacLaine

has been typecast, the way in which he projects his personality and emotions in front of the camera is an amazing achievement for a young man so lacking in experience" (*New York Post*). And Bosley Crowther in *The New York Times* said: "[Beatty], a surprising newcomer, shapes an amiable, decent, sturdy lad whose emotional exhaustion and defeat are the deep pathos in the film. Except that he talks like Marlon Brando and has some small mannerisms of James Dean, Mr. Beatty is a striking individual."

For *Roman Spring,* Beatty had made a trip to Puerto Rico, after practicing an Italian accent, to talk Tennessee Williams into giving him the role of an Italian gigolo. The story of this is told elsewhere in this book, in the section devoted to that film. This writer personally considers it Beatty's finest performance. Though reviews of the time were mixed, the film, and Beatty, have come into their own with time. Paul Beckley wrote, "Beatty plays the gigolo with an obvious appetite . . . He wheedles and poses and purrs and occasionally exposes the character's ugly interior in sharp, horrible insults." *Variety* said succinctly: "Beatty gives a fairly convincing characterization," and *Time* put it this way: "Actor Beatty plays the pretty boy for laughs as well as looks—seems as though Shirley MacLaine's little brother may be able to act after all."

Honoring his MGM commitment, Beatty repaired to that studio to make *All Fall Down,* with location scenes filmed in Key West, Florida. In this he was surrounded by such excellent performers as Angela Lansbury, Karl Malden, Eva Marie Saint and Constance Ford, in the role of a boy who brings bad luck to himself and everyone around him, especially the women. Again his reviews furthered the growth of his stellar evolution, mixed with paternal advice from such as *New Republic's* Stanley Kauffmann: "Physically, Beatty has the requisite magnetism; emotionally he has the coiled-snake tension of black lower-middle-class frustration. What he needs now, as actor, is to develop a more reliable voice, with a wider range." *The Herald-Tribune* considered Beatty's performance "the finest of his career" and *Variety* said, "He's got that undeniable star quality" while at the same time deploring his use of Dean–Brando stances and styles.

After *All Fall Down,* Beatty got out of his MGM deal, and did not appear on the nation's screens in a film for two years. He leased a pink stucco house high on top of the Strip, meditated with satisfaction on his salary increases— $15,000 for *Splendor*—$30,000 for *Roman Spring* —$60,000 for *All Fall Down.* For subsequent films, with his usual canny financial sense, he was to ask for $200,000 up—culminating in the *Bonnie and Clyde* bonanza.

At this period, six feet one inches in height, 175 pounds (he had weighed 200 in his football playing days), with a slight squint, near-sighted, thus necessitating the frequent use of thick-rimmed spectacles off-screen, he dressed casually, boasted he owned only one suit, got a reputation for being rude *and* bored during interviews, used four-letter words frequently during the same interviews, sported an offbeat sense of humor and a raucous laugh. He also had the habit of breaking up his sentences, floundering for the precise word.

He was to turn down a number of scripts in the years that followed: *Youngblood Hawke* ("I knew it was trash but I was broke and needed a new nest-egg; I finally dropped it in favor of *Lilith*— and boy, *that* was out of the frying pan into the fire!"); *PT-109* (When it was suggested he go to Washington to see President Kennedy, whom he would be portraying, to get information and soak up atmosphere, he arrogantly replied, "I don't like the script anyway, but if I do it, let him come here to California and soak up *my* atmosphere!"). He turned down dozens of scripts, later claiming he had a reputation for being "difficult" because the producers he turned down spread slanted stories about him.

He had also come to feel hatred for the Hollywood rat-race and the pressures of fame that had suddenly descended on him. "Unless I can put my heart into what I am doing, it's no good," he said, eliciting, as one writer of the time put it, "little sympathy from the millions who spend every working day doing what they don't like to do but making do with it." Of his fame he said, circa 1964: "I wasn't prepared for it—the agony, the coarseness, the vulgarity, having to do things, being pressured here, there, until finally they rub out your talent! I was insecure. I'd lost the spark. I felt as if I were being sold like a can of tomatoes."

Possibly there were attempts to sell Beatty like a can of tomatoes, considering all the admittedly commercial and trashy scripts flung at him in

1962–64, but it was also apparent that he *liked* tomatoes—all kinds—and they had, in the previous two years, included such luscious items as Joan Collins, Natalie Wood and Leslie Caron. Wood's and Caron's divorces were a result of their involvement with him, and the British director Peter Hall caused an intercontinental gossip hubbub by naming Beatty as co-respondent in his divorce suit against Miss Caron. Later Beatty, who stayed with Caron no longer than with the others, said something to the effect that he looked back on the Caron liaison "with profound sadness," as well he might have.

Beatty's compulsive womanizing was soon prime gossip-fodder for the fan magazines, and to those interviewers he could stomach with any patience, Beatty repeated over and over again, "I can't stand sustained commitment," "I'm not ready for marriage," "How can I understand anyone else when I don't yet understand myself?"

By 1967 he had taken up with Julie Christie of *Darling* (Oscar winner) and *Far from the Madding Crowd* fame, and this time he met his match in some respects, for it turned out from Miss Christie's interviews of the time that *she* didn't believe in monogamy either, nor did she think it a practical way of life—quite uncomfortable, in fact—which must have been somewhat of a relief to him.

Meanwhile Beatty continued to travel widely, have himself a good time, romance as many females as he could accommodate, take a tentative interest in politics—and occasionally try a film.

His choices for at least three years—and four

With Joan Collins

With Natalie Wood

times out—were unfortunate. *Lilith* was an unmitigated disaster. "Maybe I should have done *Youngblood Hawke* after all; it couldn't have been worse and might have been better," he joked ruefully after *Lilith* (whose director, Robert Rossen, he couldn't abide and didn't get along with) garnered such reviews as: "Rossen seems deliberately to have obscured his theme with elliptical scenes and fragmentary dialogue; as director, he has obscured his actors behind foliage, fences and fancy photography. Also it rains a lot. Because of this acute self-consciousness of style one never really gets very close to the characters." Beatty came in for his share of brickbats with Judith Crist writing: "Beatty is noteworthy for his non-

acting and his apparent inability to deliver a line without counting to ten. It's either super-Method or understandable reluctance, considering the lines."

Beatty later said of *Lilith,* which dealt with a mental hospital attendant who falls in love with a patient and later becomes as crazy as the inmates, "I tried to tell Rossen he was making a bad picture but he wouldn't pay any heed." He has said that he liked working with Rossen least of any of his directorial encounters.

Mickey One was a picture in which Beatty believed, as did director Arthur Penn. An artistic indulgence, *Mickey* made no money, was soon yanked out of circulation and has popped up occa-

With Leslie Caron

With Julie Christie at premiere of McCabe & Mrs. Miller

sionally on TV. Beatty has always defended it, telling the intelligentsia whose audience he felt warranted a look at *Mickey* to "just let it happen to you; it's on several levels, several dimensions of meaning." None of which impressed the audience he sought, who found it mannered, obscurantist and vague. "Kafka via Al Capone" was the overall reaction to this story of a Chicago nightclub comic on the lam from the Mob.

Meanwhile Beatty's romantic life kept busy as ever, with *Life*'s Tommy Thompson intoning, "With Warren Beatty there's no worry over whether seduction is possible, only when and where and who's next." Asked by another reporter if he still had ties back home in Old Virginny, he cracked, "Nope—just jackets and shirts."

The press—and the many women in his life—did give him points on one thing. He was a gentleman about talking about his love life—in fact he didn't talk about it at all. "No blabbermouth he," one reporter admitted. Meanwhile his new love, Julie Christie, continued to say things for public consumption like, "Marriage requires a special talent, like acting, like writing. I haven't got that talent, so I don't marry." To which Warren added: "Monogamy requires genius."

Two films made by Warren in 1966 did little to boost his stock. *Promise Her Anything* (a title which incidentally caused ironic laughter among his widespread circle of acquaintances) was a feeble comedy about a dirty-movie-maker, a widow (his erstwhile off-screen love, Miss Caron) and a baby. It was shot in London. The reviews tell the story on that one: "Warren Beatty is torn between dialect and vocabulary. He says his lines straight and that is bad." "Rancid twists of plot." "Mighty bumpy and frantic—obvious." *Kaleidoscope*, caper nonsense about a card cheat who marks hands for big winnings, was "frenetic, confused, inchoate, a lot of sound and fury signifying the proverbial nothing."

And then, tired of loser film fare, Beatty came home with a winner in *Bonnie and Clyde*—and the rest is film history (and financial statistics for the tax experts). *Bonnie* and the films that followed are all covered at great length in the sections devoted to them elsewhere in this book, but suffice it to say that after he talked Jack Warner into letting him produce *Bonnie* he surprised one and all with his signal success while disgusting

the more solid and conservative critics like Bosley Crowther, who deplored the film's violence and frivolous treatment of endless killings. But with *Bonnie* commencing its epic journey to a $30,-000,000-plus gross, thanks to Beatty's insistence that it open in first runs, and his constant flakking around the country for it, he became the fair-haired boy of Jack Warner, who seven years before, in 1960, had introduced Beatty to a press gathering as "one of our brightest new stars, Warner Beaker." Even Warner had not believed in *Bonnie* until late in the game. He turned up his nose at the first rushes sent him by Arthur Penn, the director, and when he was shown the entire uncut version he could only comment, "This is the longest damn movie I've ever seen!" Warner in later years liked to repeat over and over to cronies the story of how Warren went down on his knees to him to let him do the film, how he, Warner, kept backing round and round the desk "in flight from Warren Beatty's terrifying intensity."

Beatty's next film, *The Only Game in Town*, with Elizabeth Taylor, and directed by George Stevens (by then past his prime), was among other things a case of blatant miscasting; Frank Sinatra had backed out of the role after Taylor's assorted illnesses had held up production. The film, finished in early 1969, was not released for a year, what with technical difficulties and a change of personnel, "to say nothing of the fact the company realized it had a weak sister and wanted to make sure it came out in the dog-days (January-February) of 1970 so it wouldn't get in the better pictures' way," as a studio man put it.

In the 1970s Beatty's pictures have been interspersed with political excursions. In 1972 he got heavily involved in the George McGovern campaign and led a fund-raising group in Hollywood that got that unfortunate 1972 Democratic Presidential contender a great deal of monetary help. After making *McCabe & Mrs. Miller* and *$* for 1971 release (one about a whorehouse keeper in the Old West, the other about yet another bank "caper") Beatty was off the screen for nearly three years while he gave his all behind the scenes for McGovern and other Democratic political figures. In April 1972 Beatty, who campaigned that year for McGovern in more than a dozen states, masterminded a concert at Inglewood, near Hollywood, that netted McGovern some $300,000. "Essentially this is a way of countering the

With Lillian Hellman

money raised by big individual contributors on the old side of the party," Beatty said at the time. "What we're really talking about is money." On hand to pitch in for the cause were singer-actress Barbra Streisand, Carole King, James Taylor, and composer Quincy Jones. The fund-raising event sold out 16,000 seats of the Inglewood forum in eighteen hours.

Of his activities in this area Beatty has said, "You have to pull in and out of politics, otherwise you can exhaust yourself, particularly if you're not a professional. You can wind up very resentful. It's hard to see results in politics. Years ago, when Bobby and King and everybody was shot, Senator Joe Tydings introduced a bill on gun control. The polls were 85 percent in favor, but it got totally watered down." His lip curled in disgust at the thought. "Movies are more fulfilling than politics, I have found," he added. "Let's face it, politics is constant compromise. Art should never be. But that prompts a conversation on whether a thing that costs a lot and has a group of people working harassed schedules should be called art or near-art. It's a hell of a lot easier to see results in movies. I think I'm temperamentally closer to art, but I'm not sure about either. I can say what I have to say in films. In politics, I feel that compromise keeps you from it."

In retrospect, he still feels so keenly the pain of Nixon's 1968 victory that he brings it up at every opportunity and even made it part of the background for *Shampoo*, eliciting what some critics called "a bid for cheap snickers." Earlier, he had helped the American Civil Liberties Union raise money to work on Proposition 9 (the fund-raising issue). Always he has repeated, "I'll help wher-

With Michelle Phillips and her daughter

Receiving the Harvard Hasty Pudding Theatricals Award

ever I'm needed in the political sphere if it doesn't take me away too much from whatever film I'm currently engaged on."

His political interests were reflected in *The Parallax View* (1974) which investigates the truth behind the assassination of a political candidate.

In February 1976 it was announced in *The New York Times* that Beatty was considering entering a number of big state Democratic primaries as a "surrogate" for a Democratic ticket headed by Senator Hubert Humphrey of Minnesota for President and Senator Edward M. Kennedy of Massa-

chusetts for Vice President. Christopher Lydon of the *Times* reported: "As the impresario of some hugely successful celebrity fund-raising concerts for the George McGovern Presidential campaign in 1972, Mr. Beatty's popular touch and strategic imagination are taken seriously enough by Democratic professionals for him to have been courted by several of the active candidates, including Senator Henry M. Jackson of Washington and former Governor Jimmy Carter of Georgia."

In a telephone interview with the *Times* at that point, Beatty covered at length the idea of a political stand-in role and spoke specifically about putting his name on the ballot in California, Ohio and New Jersey primaries and possibly others. Of these projected moves he said:

"I can see it as somewhat of an expression of resistance to the primary system itself, and as an expression of frustration at the fact that the leadership of the Democratic Party—Kennedy, Humphrey, Muskie, McGovern and others—are not participating in the primaries."

In 1975 two Beatty films were released, *Shampoo,* which grossed a cool 30 million dollars in its first three months alone, according to *Variety,* and *The Fortune,* a spoof about a kidnap "caper," 1930s-style, and co-starring another Hollywood Winner of the 1970s, Jack Nicholson. More about these two films in the sections in this book devoted to them, but suffice it to say that the Roman Catholic Church got after *Shampoo,* giving it a "condemned" rating from the U.S. Catholic Conference and finding it morally objectionable *in toto* for Roman Catholics. The Conference's film and broadcasting division gave *Shampoo* the "C"

rating—the toughest of its classifications—and asserted that *Shampoo*'s people, including Beatty, Goldie Hawn, his erstwhile love Julie Christie and others, were "beautiful to watch, even though they go through some of the ugliest situations and raunchiest dialogue seen outside hard-core theatres."

While the Catholic clout isn't as hard on the movie business as it was in the halcyon '30s and '40s, when the Legion of Decency and the Production Code held forth, some wonder if Catholic condemnation of his mammoth moneymaker will reflect in any way on Beatty's future ability to maneuver politically in a Democratic Party which numbers Catholics heavily among its multitudes.

In 1976 Beatty had announced as his next film project a biography of John Reed, the young Harvard radical and Village leftist of fifty years ago who went to Russia, wrote *Ten Days that Shook the World,* and died there, getting himself buried beside the Kremlin Wall with other Soviet he-

roes. Beatty talked to those who knew Reed, including the late Walter Lippmann. "I was going to make it in Russia," Beatty later said. "I was very enthusiastic about it and all set to go, but when I thought about the Russians invading Czechoslovakia I pulled away from it." After that, he said, "I sort of relaxed and thought, 'What am I really running after? Why don't I just relax and have some fun?' I decided to do more studying and living and to pay more attention to American politics."

His next movie brainstorm was "a super-elegant porno movie" production, costs for which would run into many millions, but he was talked out of that one when he went as a delegate for Governor Brown to the Democratic National Convention (he had switched from his idol Ted Kennedy when he knew Kennedy definitely wouldn't run in 1976). His fellow "pols" intoned, "If you want to get ahead in politics, nix on the porno." After that he toyed with the idea of doing a movie on the late Howard Hughes, with himself as Hughes of course, but that too fell through, for reasons never satisfactorily explained publicly.

He finally elected to do *Heaven Can Wait,* a rewrite by Elaine May of the highly successful Robert Montgomery–Evelyn Keyes–Claude Rains *Here Comes Mr. Jordan* (1941), with Beatty as director, producer and star. Warners had nixed the project because of the six-million-dollar budget estimate on the film (which had also served as a Rita Hayworth 1947 Columbia vehicle, *Down to Earth*). Paramount finally went along with a deal, and production commenced there in the summer of 1977, with a February 1978 release projected. Buck Henry helped Beatty with the directorial chores, and in the cast were Julie Christie, Dyan Cannon, Charles Grodin, James Mason and Vincent Gardenia. Beatty had tried to persuade Cary Grant to come out of retirement to play the "heavenly messenger" Rains had made famous, but Grant declined. A fey romantic comedy about an athlete who dies too soon and is returned to earth, it represents yet another departure for Beatty. A September 1977 news report had all the cast feuding with each other on the set, with Dyan Cannon wanting alphabetical billing in the credits and Julie Christie objecting. According to the *New York Post*: "Julie and Warren aren't speaking either, and you'd never know they were once lovers. Warren isn't speaking to his co-director Buck Henry, co-

With Carol Haney in A Loss of Roses

star Charles Grodin isn't speaking to anybody. James Mason, who plays God (in a revamp of the old Rains role) is staying above it all." After many production vicissitudes, *Heaven* got itself released in the summer of 1978—and proved a smash financial hit.

As of 1979 Beatty's love life continues to sell magazines and move newspapers. For a while he moved back and forth bewilderingly between Christie and Michelle Phillips and dallied with a couple of opera singers and assorted young ladies who crossed his path. Phillips had ended her affair with him—for a time—in 1976 and moved herself and her five-year-old daughter out of the house she shared with Beatty in Beverly Hills. Miss Phillips was the former wife of John Phil-

lips, father of her child, who had once sung with her in the Mamas and Papas group. Phillips went on to play Natacha Rambova in Rudy Nureyev's Ken Russell–directed *Valentino.* Warren went on to get himself linked with such disparate ladies as Brooke Hayward (author of *Haywire*) and even Jacqueline Kennedy Onassis herself. His current protracted dalliance has been with actress Diane Keaton.

But whatever the current state of his activities in finance, politics, films and the Wonderful World of Woman, it can safely be said that in his own style and in his own fashion, Mr. Warren Beatty has made the All-American Dream come true.

The Films of
WARREN BEATTY

Splendor in the Grass

CAST:
Natalie Wood *(Wilma Dean Loomis);* Warren Beatty *(Bud Stamper);* Pat Hingle *(Ace Stamper);* Audrey Christie *(Mrs. Loomis);* Barbara Loden *(Ginny Stamper);* Fred Stewart *(Del Loomis);* Zohra Lampert *(Angelina);* Joanna Roos *(Mrs. Stamper);* Jan Norris *(Juanita Howard);* Gary Lockwood *(Toots);* Sandy Dennis *(Kay);* Crystal Field *(Hazel);* Marla Adams *(June);* Lynn Loring *(Carolyn);* John McGovern *(Doc Smiley);* Martine Bartlett *(Miss Metcalf);* Sean Garrison *(Glenn);* Charles Robinson *(Johnny Masterson);* Phyllis Diller *(Texas Guinan);* William Inge *(Reverend Whitman);* Phoebe Mackay *(Stamper servant).*

Advertisement for Splendor in the Grass

CREDITS:
An NBI Picture. Elia Kazan *(Producer and Director)*; William Inge *(Screenplay)*; Boris Kaufman *(Photography)*; David Amram *(Music Composer and Conductor)*; Richard Sylbert *(Production Designer)*; Gene Callahan *(Set Decorator)*; Gene Milford *(Editor)*; Edward Johnstone *(Sound)*; William Inge and Charles H. Maguire *(Associate Producers)*; Don Kranze *(Assistant Director)*; Anna H. Johnstone *(Costumes)*; Robert Jiras *(Makeup)*; Willis Hanchett *(Hairstyles)*; George Tapps *(Choreographer)*. Color by Technicolor.

Opened at the Victoria Theatre, New York, October 10, 1961. Running time, 124 minutes.

William Inge was the man who made possible the film debut of Warren Beatty. Beatty had made a Broadway splash in Inge's *A Loss of Roses,* a short-lived, late-1959 play which in turn had resulted from the discovery of Beatty in a North Jersey playhouse by Inge and Joshua Logan. Within a few months of the play's closing, Inge had succeeded in getting Beatty the lead in the first work Inge had ever written expressly for films, *Splendor in the Grass.* Inge, of *Bus Stop, Picnic* and *Dark at the Top of the Stairs* fame, had come up with a poignant story of youthful frustrations in 1929 Kansas. Heavily edited, then produced and directed by Elia Kazan, who had done such brilliant work in adapting Tennessee Williams' work to the stage, the film was one of the big hits of 1961. It had been photographed a full year before its release, in mid-1960.

During an interview with Natalie Wood on the set of the film in 1960, she told me: "Elia Kazan is most exciting to work with. He's an education for any actor. He cuts right through to the core of a characterization. And with Kazan, there are never any waits between scenes. He keeps us all busy, going over lines, trying new things with each scene. It's the most creative experience I've ever had."

Splendor in the Grass was also the film that brought about the beginning of the end of her first marriage to Robert Wagner (they remarried many years later), for during it she fell in love with her young co-star, Warren Beatty. Formal separation from Wagner did not come for months afterwards, after which Wood and Beatty were constantly together—while it lasted. Wood re-

Beatty and Natalie Wood in the Flush of First Love

Crystal Field tries the vamp act on Beatty.

59

called that Kazan had worked very hard to help Beatty give credibility, point and sharpness to his performance. It was Beatty's first film role and he was, she recalls, understandably nervous and unsure, fussing over his appearance with mirrors (a habit Kazan corrected in short order) and expressing continual doubts as to the effectiveness of his scenes. He need not have worried, for upon the Fall 1961 release of *Splendor*, he found himself a major star.

Since every young actor who got his head above the crowd circa 1961 found himself inevitably compared with Brando, Clift and above all, Dean, Beatty came in for his share of such flak; some critics insisted he looked like Dean. He did tend to copy some of Dean's squinting mannerisms and shambling stances, though this may have been unconscious with him. He was also nearsighted and used his unusually small eyes in a piercing, staring manner that often degenerated into a squint, with disconcerting frequency. But there was no denying the power of his performance. The voice of this new twenty-four-year-old may have reminded some of Brando's but the personality was distinctively his own.

Splendor was the first of the three early films that during a release period of seven months (October 1961 to May 1962) made Warren Beatty the latest household name among film enthusiasts. The other two were *The Roman Spring of Mrs. Stone*, released in December 1961, and *All Fall Down*, released in 1962. *Mrs. Stone* was based on a Tennessee Williams novel, while *All Fall Down* was a William Inge screenplay of a James Leo Herlihy novel. In all three, Beatty was cast to perfection. In *Splendor* Beatty was playing a character he understood and heavily identified with; he was moreover cast in a film that reflected the individualized insights and inner processes of an original artist, Inge, and he was guided by the

Beatty and Wood argue while they walk.

sensitive Kazan, who understood so well the deep wells of the human heart and the force of individual passions. How could Beatty fail? He didn't—and he was the Star Find of 1961.

It is interesting to compare the first three Beatty films of 1961–62 with the first three of James Dean in 1955–56. We will never know how Dean might have matured as artist and man; we do know what happened to Beatty, now forty-two and a veteran of a surprisingly few fifteen films in seventeen years. Dean achieved his magical effects by playing characters he understood, people either identically, or much like, his private persona. Beatty did likewise. It is now—and always will be—a matter of speculation whether Dean would have stayed close to type in what would now have been a twenty-four-year career, or whether, like Beatty, he would have deserted the persona and image that made him initially famous for variegated roles—in Beatty's case not

always well-advised, considering that he was a definite *but* limited talent who depended for his prime effects on projections of his deeper self.

Beatty put into his role of Bud Stamper all the repressed passion, all the rebellion, all the hurt and confusion that he had known in his Virginia childhood and adolescence. He was twenty-three in 1960, and his memories of that fallow period of his life were still fresh, so his perceptions of Bud Stamper's character flowed from a wellspring of youthful enthusiasm and subconscious purgation. It could not be said of Beatty that what he projected in *Splendor* was exactly "emotion recollected in tranquillity." Rather it was emotion—in actuality only five years or so in the past—recollected with an intensity of purgation, a tense "sloughing-off-of-the-dross" that emerged kinetic and fierce on the screen—passionate, tender, feelingful and eloquent.

To this writer, *The Roman Spring of Mrs. Stone*

Family tension at the dinner table with sister Barbara Loden and mother Joanna Roos

Wood and Beatty find love beautiful — and terrifying.

Crystal Field gives Beatty the waterfall-seduction treatment.

demonstrates Beatty's peculiar artistry to maximum effect. But *Splendor* (and in another context *All Fall Down*) gives us the Beatty purging his early hurts, working through all the pain of his difficult early growth — growing pains with the accent on *pains*. Beatty, like many another great star, *played himself* in *Splendor,* and through the art of Inge, the insights of Kazan, he found his catharsis, his liberation from a painful past, and the entrance, via stardom, into a new life of freedom and self-realization.

No twenty-three-year-old artist-in-the-making could have had a more fortunate vehicle with which to be introduced to the film public. *Splendor in the Grass* is a masterpiece — sensitive, tender, searing, brutal in its exposition of small-town stupidity and narrowness, 1928–30 style, but deeply understanding of its people — a film with no heroes or villains, just people, victims not merely of fate or circumstances but of their own weaknesses — and their misplaced ideals. Miss Wood plays like a poetess, sensitive and delicate as Wilma Loomis, a nice girl with the best intentions who loves Beatty and he her. They want to keep their love "pure" and "fine," so they resist the temptation to sexual experimentation. But the strain of sexual abstention, the stupid, benighted, puritanical parental attitudes they encounter, the lack of understanding from all about them, drive them finally into illness and moral breakdown for Beatty, heartbreak, frustration and all-out madness for Wood. *Splendor* is the tragedy of two young people, finer and rarer than most, whose very decency is their undoing, surrounded as they are by *in*sensitive, *in*decent, hypocritical relatives and friends.

The screenplay is said to have been based on an incident in William Inge's own youth. Since that late sensitive artist's private life is fairly well known, it must have been a traumatic experience indeed for him. For into *Splendor,* Inge, aided by Kazan's sharp illuminations, put a painfully evident degree of his own lifetime of hurt, loneliness, and isolation, which produced much of the turmoil of mind and heart and soul that his two young protagonists had to suffer. Passion banked, love denied, two "sensitives" at bay before the "insensitives" around them — so much of the rare and beautiful spirit of William Inge, all his life's sufferings, all his profound hurts, are in that film.

And because Inge was a *true* artist, he *univer-*

salized his symbols of suffering, and we find much of ourselves in the tragic Bud and Wilma.

The film is uncommonly well acted, beautifully photographed (locations were shot in Staten Island and High Falls, New York) by Boris Kaufman and scored evocatively by David Amram, who obviously comprehended the period and ambience with which he was dealing.

Audrey Christie is the Monster Midwest Mother personified—neurotic, soggily sentimental yet cruelly obtuse. Fred Stewart gives a sensitively understated portrait of the long-suffering husband of a termagant. Pat Hingle is the big-business, small-soul obtuse daddy to the core and his scenes with son Beatty, in which he drains the life out him just as Wood's mother drains *her* life, are graphic, indeed horrifying. Barbara Loden gives a shrill, at times terrifying, impersonation of Beatty's sister who is as unrestrained and amoral as her brother is self-respecting and idealistic.

One of the film's most moving scenes comes when she fights his efforts to keep her from going out with a "wrong guy." When Loden sees the loneliness and frustration in her idealistic brother's face, his desire to do the right thing, she experiences a momentary attack of conscience that is moving to watch.

Natalie Wood is profoundly touching as she wilts under the knowledge that Beatty has left her for the school tart because he cannot stand the frustration of their unfulfilled love. Gradually she slides into madness, and when she goes to pieces while soaking in a bathtub and shrieks out her despair at her mother's puritanical concern with her being "spoiled," she is wildly eloquent indeed. So is Beatty as he tries to get help from the town doctor, as he all but weeps while his obtuse father tells him to find "another type of girl" for a sexual outlet. And Gary Lockwood, to whom Wood turns for temporary consolation,

Beatty and mother Joanna Roos cope with their eccentrically macho paterfamilias, Pat Hingle, as best they can.

limns all the stupid, insensitive teen tomcats of time immemorial as he tries to provide lustful escapism as a tawdry substitute for the totally fulfilled mutual love Wood craves with Beatty alone.

Beatty's tears against the hospital wall after his love has gone all-out mad and is moaning in a nearby hospital room are the finest expression of teenage despair in this or any picture. Then it's off to Yale, where he fails. His father kills himself after the Crash, his sister is killed in a car accident, and he ends up on a farm with a second-best choice, Zohra Lampert, and a baby. When she comes out of the sanitarium, Wood, who is to marry a young doctor she met there, goes to see her love for one last time. And as they face each other, in some of the most eloquently restrained and poetically understated closing scenes of film history, she realizes that "though nothing can bring back the hour of splendor in the grass, glory in the flower" they should and must "grieve not, rather find, strength in what remains behind. . . ."

Splendor in the Grass is a film masterpiece that will endure—and no young actor could have asked for a more impressive debut-vehicle.

REVIEWS:
Bosley Crowther in *The New York Times:*
"A frank and ferocious social drama that makes the eyes pop and the modest cheek burn . . . sex and parental domineering are made to appear congenital forces that misshape the lives of two nice kids, played with amazing definition by Warren Beatty and Natalie Wood . . . The torment of two late-adolescents, yearning yet not daring to love, is played against the harsh backdrop of cheapness, obtuseness and hypocrisy in a socially isolated Kansas town of the 1920s . . . the authority and eloquence of the theme emerge in the honest, sensitive acting of Mr. Beatty and Miss Wood.

Family doctor John McGovern, dad Pat Hingle,
and Beatty confer over Natalie Wood's nervous breakdown.

The former, a surprising newcomer, shapes an amiable, decent, sturdy lad whose emotional exhaustion and defeat are the deep pathos in the film. Except that he talks like Marlon Brando and has some small mannerisms of James Dean, Mr. Beatty is a striking individual. And Miss Wood has a beauty and radiance that carry through a role of violent passions and depressions with unsullied purity and strength."

Time:
"Actor Beatty, who at twenty-four is playing his first screen part of any account, should make the big time on the first bounce. In the matter of talent, sister Shirley MacLaine can give him cards and spades, but he has a startling resemblance to the late James Dean, and he has that certain something Hollywood calls star quality. . . . Actress Wood is quietly adroit and appealing."

Paul V. Beckley in *The New York Herald Tribune:*
"One of the strongest American films of the year . . . Inge's style and Kazan's direction obviously suit actors, for the film is alive with fine performances . . . it also proves the maturity of Miss Wood as an actress . . . Warren Beatty's performance, too, reflects a maturity that is as cheering as Miss Wood's . . . the denouement, the final meeting of the ill-fated young lovers, is the best example of Inge's, Kazan's and the actors' gifts for restrained, subtle and yet powerful expression."

Variety:
"Poignant, romantic drama . . . a very human, personal story with a timeless, uplifting theme . . . Natalie Wood and Warren Beatty are the lovers. Although the range and amplitude of their expression is not always as wide and variable as

Beatty and dad Pat Hingle in the midst of some boozy kitchen fun.

it might be, both deliver convincing, appealing performances."

Films in Review:
"Inge's original intention may have been to etch a vignette of Kansas life in the '20s, but what has been put on the screen is merely a truckling to Hollywood's present conception of how to make money, i.e., tell teenagers that fathers are either dominating or hen-pecked nitwits; that mothers are neurotics; and that the adult world isn't worth the powder to blow it to hell. How much of this dreariness is Inge, and how much Kazan, I do not know . . . there are good as well as bad performances. Natalie Wood is rather good, but Warren Beatty is too inexperienced to be able to project *anything*. I am told Hollywood hopes to make him a star, but his face, at least in this picture, is on the weak side, and doesn't always photograph well."

Family portrait, Midwest-1928 style: Mother Joanna Roos, dad Pat Hingle, sister Barbara Loden (making with the derrick) wince for the birdie.

Beatty tries to explain his adolescent needs and hungers to dad Pat Hingle.

The Roman Spring of Mrs. Stone

CAST:
Vivien Leigh *(Karen Stone)*; Warren Beatty *(Paolo)*; Lotte Lenya *(The Contessa)*; Coral Browne *(Meg)*; Jill St. John *(Barbara)*; Jeremy Spenser *(The Young Man)*; Stella Bonheur *(Mrs. Jamison-Walker)*; Josephine Brown *(Lucia)*; Peter Dyneley *(Greener)*; Carl Jaffe *(The Baron)*; Harold Kasket *(Tailor)*; Viola Keats *(Julia)*; Cleo Laine *(Singer)*; Bessie Love *(Bunny)*; Elspeth March *(Mrs. Barrow)*; Henry McCarthy *(Kennedy)*; Warren Mitchell *(Giorgio)*; John Phillips *(Tom Stone)*; Paul Stassino *(Barber)*; Ernest Thesiger *(Stefano)*; Mavis Villiers *(Mrs. Coogan)*; Thelma d'Agular *(Mita)*.

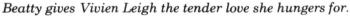

Beatty gives Vivien Leigh the tender love she hungers for.

Gigolo Beatty and procuress Lotte Lenya get nasty with each other.

CREDITS:
A Seven Arts Presentation. Louis de Rochemont *(Producer);* José Quintero *(Director);* Gavin Lambert *(Screenplay);* Based on the novel by Tennessee Williams; Harry Waxman *(Photography);* Richard Addinsell *(Music);* Douglas Gamley *(Music Conductor);* Song, "Che Noia L'Amor," lyrics by Paddy Roberts *(Sung by Cleo Laine);* Herbert Smith *(Art Director);* John Jarvis *(Set Decorator);* Roger Furse *(Production Designer);* Ralph Kamplen *(Editor);* Cecil Mason *(Sound);* Balmain *(Miss Leigh's Gowns);* B. Dawson *(Costumes);* Lothar Wolff *(Associate Producer);* Basil Somner *(Production Manager);* Peter Yates *(Assistant Director).* Color by Technicolor.

Opened at the Capitol and Trans-Lux 85th Street Theatres, New York, December 28, 1961. Running time, 104 minutes.

Tennessee Williams, on whose novel *The Roman Spring of Mrs. Stone* was based, has expressed his admiration for the film version in his *Memoirs,* calling it "a poem." His admiration for its star, Vivien Leigh, is also evident, and he has made the uniquely arresting observation concerning her that, having experienced the outer reaches of madness in her personal life, she understood death and was prepared for it when it came for her in 1967, six years after *Mrs. Stone,* which was her next-to-last picture. But of Warren Beatty, her co-star, Williams says nothing.

Beatty has often told of how he carefully studied an Italian accent that he felt would suffice for the role of Paolo, the Italian gigolo of aristocratic origin who insinuates himself into the life of the lonely expatriate American actress, Mrs. Stone, in Rome, and eventually contributes to his fifty-year-old inamorata's ruin. He has also detailed

Beatty is initially puzzled by Leigh's mysterious reserve.

Leigh and Beatty get to know each other in gradual stages.

his efforts to get Williams to accept him in the part. Beatty had already won the approval of Miss Leigh and director José Quintero, who was essaying the movies after stage triumphs with *The Iceman Cometh* and other plays. But Williams had let it be known that he wanted an Italian actor for Paolo, also someone older than Beatty's then twenty-three years. Beatty went down to Puerto Rico uninvited, to see Williams and persuade him that he was right for the role. There seems to be a persistent mystery as to what exactly transpired between the ambitious twenty-three-year-old and the jaded, sybaritic, emotionally mercurial playwright of forty-eight. The sojourn in Puerto Rico has come out in bits and pieces over the years. Beatty says he found Williams in a gambling casino, and walked right up to him and began talking in what he felt was a convincing Italian dialect. Williams, who had never laid eyes on him before, took him for an Italian on face value, and when Beatty later con-

fessed his identity, he had a head start in persuading Williams to approve him for the role of Paolo.

Beatty also told interviewers that Williams was "set in his ways, like a lot of older people are." Williams reportedly told friends that Beatty won his point because his general behavior in Puerto Rico made it obvious that he had all the required instincts for delivering Paolo to screen audiences in a convincing manner—a double-edged observation if ever there was one.

And so, with the playwright's approval, Beatty winged to London and Rome to display himself, with leer, tight pants and sexy posturings, in a picture that, alone of all the fifteen Beatty movies I have seen to date, convinces me that there is an artist somewhere underneath the elusive façade of most Beatty screen performances. As I wrote of his performance in *The Great Romantic Films,* he plays "a ruthless narcissist rendered irredeemably cynical by childhood sufferings during World

Beatty lashes back at Leigh's scorn for his new white suit.

War II. He is a predator and revenge-seeker who senses that in Mrs. Stone he has a subconsciously amenable victim. . . . It remains one of the interesting oddities of screen acting that he was never again so subtly fine. One explanation might be that the sensuality, the slyness, the predatory, feel-for-the-soft-spots insensitivity and atavism of Paolo had in them elements akin to aspects of Beatty's private nature. And in this one film in which he displayed himself an artist, they served Beatty well."

Considering that he led a well-publicized existence as a heterosexual stud of voracious needs with a variety of ladies, even at that time, it is oddly interesting that Beatty's acting should be at its best in milieus—and among people—of homosexual or bisexual persuasion. In the creative conceptions of homosexual writers, Beatty always seemed to shine; in oddly ambivalent, velvety, indeed lavenderish, ambiences, the artist in Beatty seemed to emerge more clearly. The impotence and suspected homosexual leanings of Clyde Barrow gave an added edge to his *Bonnie and Clyde* performance; *Shampoo,* in which he was determined to smash the "myth" as he conceived it, of Don Juan hetero wolves sublimating a homo complex, was another highlight for him. And he made his initial impact in *Splendor in the Grass,* a 1961 film which to sophisticated 1979 eyes, seems more the memories of a repressed gay's childhood than a depiction of 1928 hetero doings in a stultifying small-town Kansas atmosphere.

Be all that as it may, Beatty in *Roman Spring of Mrs. Stone,* gave what many consider his best performance. It was all the more amazing a tour de force in that he was a former football-playing Virginian who had sought to come on as American as Apple Pie—and here he was, with Italian accent, essaying a sleek cougar in a decadent Tennessee Williams study of Roman gigolos and the women (and men) on whom they preyed. Since Williams had spent some time in Rome, and knew the hustler scene very well, *Mrs. Stone,* like Inge's *Splendor,* seemed to be homosexual life masquerading for public consumption as a more shady side of the hetero life style. And in it, to repeat, All-American-Boy-Macho Beatty was surprisingly in his element.

Miss Leigh at forty-eight was already jaded, cynical, tired of life, disillusioned; Laurence Olivier had left her for a younger woman; she was the kind of person who did not take well to aging, and as the desperate, widowed, defensively proud yet love-hungry and emotionally vulnerable retired actress, she was as convincing in her interpretation as Beatty was in his.

The Roman Spring of Mrs. Stone is certainly a work of film art that looks better and better with time. José Quintero directed with great sensitivity and an authentic feel for his subject; Richard Addinsell's inspired music provided just the right background; and Harry Waxman's Technicolor photography was perfect in its evocation, in subdued, subtle hues, of the decadent counterpoint of the emotional situations evoked. And Lotte Lenya as the procuress gave a deliciously sinuous and serpentine performance that complemented the Leigh and Beatty thespian doings admirably. Years later, I told Miss Lenya of my admiration for this performance, which should have won her an Oscar. She recalled that Miss Leigh was a wistful figure at this stage of her career, none too happy, and that she, Miss Lenya, felt a great sympathy for her during the shooting. The two women's scenes together, with Lenya trying to force money from Leigh for having arranged the original introduction to Beatty, is thespic chess-playing of the first water. Jeremy Spenser is sinister and ominously graphic as the strange young man who follows Mrs. Stone around Rome and stands beneath her window gesturing up to her. When Beatty, after dallying with Leigh for as long as he can get things out of her, leaves her for a movie actress (Jill St. John) who offers better financial pickings, Leigh, in the now-famous closing scene, throws her keys down to Spenser, who comes up to her apartment and presumably puts an end, once and for all, to her humiliations and torments. This is implied by the way his coat fills the screen as he advances toward her while she waits calmly for what is, in effect, her suicide.

The film is full of inimitable verbal gems only Williams could have inspired, though the screenplay was done by Gavin Lambert, who preserved the Williams spirit to the best of his ability. The picture is an expansion and elaboration of the rather slight novel, and the literate and polished but tastefully self-effacing Lambert gave it an unmistakable Williams flavor. And those lines! "The beautiful make their own laws," Leigh tells Lenya. At another point she disarms Lenya's sar-

A happy moment for Leigh and Beatty on t[he] patio overlooking Rome

castic hints about her vulnerability by saying, "Americans are not as romantic as their motion pictures." And when she expresses her middle-aged jealousy of her younger rival to Beatty, he turns on her contemptuously with the words: "Rome is 3,000 years old — how old are you, fifty?" The cat-and-mouse counterpoint between jaded, aware, yet romantically vulnerable Leigh and predatory, narcissistic, ruthlessly destructive Beatty is something to see, and is as fresh today as when it was made. When Beatty tries to intimidate her by telling of a middle-aged woman found in bed with her throat cut, Leigh faces him down across the card table with the words: "After three more years of this, a cut throat would be a convenience."

The film is full of sardonic, bitchy exchanges dear to the conceptions of a certain type of homosexual. When dizzy-yet-catty young movie actress Jill St. John tells Leigh, "I'm afraid I've never seen you in a play," Leigh replies crisply: "*I'm* afraid I've never seen *you* in the movies."

Procuress Lenya's scenes with her other "clients" are what the gays would term "camp screams." Dealing with a female client of "regular" sexual needs and a Baron who obviously wants a young male of a certain stripe, Lenya purrs: "I will be able to help you very soon, Madame, but for you, Baron, it will take a little longer."

A decadent, bittersweet, flawless example of decadent romanticism, Williams style, *The Roman Spring of Mrs. Stone* has picked up a sophisticated, esthetically aware cult audience in the decade and a half since it was made, and director José Quintero, whose career has had its ups and downs since, can take satisfaction in the knowledge that this is as representative a masterpiece of his as it is of Williams.

Many have speculated since 1961 as to why Beatty wanted the role so badly. Obviously it was because he wanted a change of pace from the stultifying 1928-style Americanisms of *Splendor in the Grass* and felt that playing an Italian gigolo convincingly would attest to his virtuosity, which it did. Also, I suspect that subconsciously he wanted to escape to Europe and another culture and totally different life-style, if only cinemati-

A moment of truth for the unhappy pair

cally, as another step in his constant, though not always conscious, efforts to get away from that lonely, stultifying and convention-ridden Virginia childhood and youth.

Had Beatty continued to essay exotic roles that suited his inner escape schematics, he might have had a far more prestigious career since *Mrs. Stone.* For no matter how much he may enjoy the posturings of the All-American Boy, All-American Boy he isn't, nor ever was.

REVIEWS:

"Tube" in *Variety:*
"Miss Leigh gives an expressive, interesting delineation—projecting intelligence and femininity—as always. Mrs. Stone, however, is no Blanche DuBois. There's less to work with. Although every once in a while a little Guido Panzini creeps into his Italo dialect and Marlon Brando into his posture and expression, Beatty gives a fairly convincing characterization . . . Miss Lenya, the noted German actress, is frighteningly sinister as the cunning pimpette—an excellent portrayal. Top supporting roles are capably executed . . . Alert, inventive direction by Quintero is helpful throughout. His prologue, or pre-title, scenes are especially well-handled . . . topnotch camera work . . . Richard Addinsell's melancholy score is another valuable ingredient."

Time:
"Actress Leigh comes out of it with laurels refreshed and a new screen career before her . . . Actor Beatty plays the pretty boy for laughs as well as looks—seems as though Shirley MacLaine's little brother may be able to act after all."

Films in Review:
"Warren Beatty [plays] the male whore. Because I am unfamiliar with such lowlife, I suppose, he seemed well cast to me, though it's true his Italian accent kept slipping. At least his dead-pan face was appropriate in this degraded role . . .

soap opera by Tennessee Williams . . . You may like male whores in your soap operas but movies like this one are making me sigh for radio's good old Helen Trent . . . such subject matter is what one expects from Williams, and seems the sort of material suitable to a screenwriter such as Gavin Lambert. And José Quintero also seems the right director for it. Vivien Leigh [is] well-cast . . . still quite beautiful, in certain lighting, from the right angles."

Paul V. Beckley in *The New York Herald Tribune:*
"[The film] isn't altogether palatable, but it is honestly and carefully made . . . the slightly sweet smell of decay hovers over everything. Although its very subject matter limits this film and smothers it slightly, it is quietly and sincerely made and Vivien Leigh gives a striking performance . . . it has a fine finish and the color is good . . . Beatty plays the gigolo with an obvious appetite. He wheedles and poses and purrs and occasionally exposes the character's ugly interior in sharp, horrible insults."

Arthur Knight in *The Saturday Review:*
". . . Decadence itself can be quite fascinating, and especially when the decadents are such beautiful people as Vivien Leigh and Warren Beatty. Physically, the production is impeccable—as polished, sleek and handsome as the star herself. The story, on the other hand, is like an Albright canvas, where mouldering flesh is set against glistening silks and gleaming satins . . . Tennessee Williams has never posed either as a psychologist or an anthropologist; he is a humanist, dredging the dark and secret places of the heart."

Bosley Crowther in *The New York Times:*
"[Miss Leigh's] surges of ardor have the fullness and fitfulness of the real thing; her torrents of grief are as liquid as though they came from a heart truly crushed."

All Fall Down

CAST:

Eva Marie Saint *(Echo O'Brien)*; Warren Beatty *(Berry-Berry Willart)*; Karl Malden *(Ralph Willart)*; Angela Lansbury *(Annabel Willart)*; Brandon De Wilde *(Clinton Willart)*; Constance Ford *(Mrs. Mandel)*; Barbara Baxley *(Schoolteacher)*; Evans Evans *(Hedy)*; Jennifer Howard *(Myra)*; Madame Spivy *(Bouncer)*; Albert Paulson *(Captain Ramirez)*; Henry Kulky *(Sailor)*; Colette Jackson *(Dorothy)*; Robert Sorrells *(Waiter in Sweet Shop)*; Bernadette Withers *(Mildred)*; Carol Kelly *(Flame)*; Paul Bryar *(Sweet Shop Manager)*.

CREDITS:

John Houseman *(Producer)*; John Frankenheimer *(Director)*; William Inge *(Screenplay)*; Based on the novel by James Leo Herlihy; Lionel Lindon *(Photographer)*; Alex North *(Music)*; George W. Davis and Preston Ames *(Art Directors)*; Henry Grace and George R. Nelson *(Set Decorations)*; Robert R. Hoag *(Special Visual Effects)*; Frederic Steinkamp *(Editor)*; Franklin Milton *(Recording Supervisor)*; Dorothy Jeakins *(Costumes)*; William Tuttle *(Makeup)*; Sydney Guilaroff *(Hair Styles)*; Ethel Winant *(Associate Producer)*; Hal Polaire *(Assistant Director)*.

Opened at Loew's State Theatre, New York, April 11, 1962. Running time, 111 minutes.

All Fall Down showcases Beatty in one of his more effective performances, and it is my per-

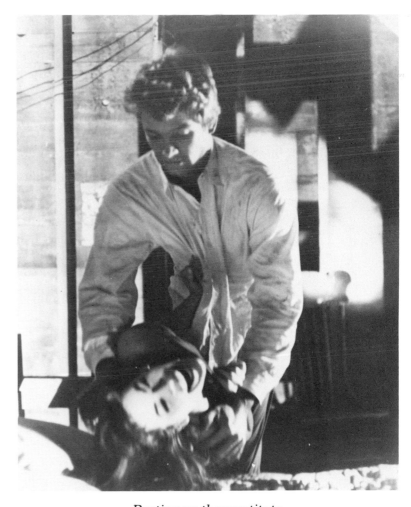

Beating up the prostitute.

His loving, trusting brother, Brandon De Wilde, offers money.

Demonstrating to De Wilde his power over women

Beatty brings love's ecstasies to Eva Marie Saint.

sonal third-favorite Beatty portrayal (after *Roman Spring of Mrs. Stone* and *Splendor in the Grass,* in that order). Once again the fast-rising young star enjoyed the expert character delineations of William Inge, with Inge basing his screenplay on the novel of another "sensitive," James Leo Herlihy, later of *Midnight Cowboy* fame. As before noted, it is esthetically of interest that "sensitives" Williams and Inge could get to the essence of Beatty's mystique as an actor and bring out the best in him. Inge had tapped depths in Beatty in his first film; all the adolescent rebellion and stultification of purpose and desire that he endured in *Splendor* was reflective of elements in Beatty's Virginia youth, hence at twenty-three

he had a subject, a theme and an ambience with which he could identify wholeheartedly, and with young enthusiasm and inspiration. Williams's *Roman Spring* had represented the morbidly escapist aspect, into another world, forbidden, exotic, outré, that Beatty had also doubtless fantasized in that repressed Virginia youth.

And now in *All Fall Down,* Inge, and Herlihy in his original novel, again provided Beatty with a character he intuitively understood.

Much has been made of Beatty's being in the Dean-Brando-Clift tradition (it is interesting to speculate what might have happened to *Beatty's* legend had he died in 1962 at twenty-five right after the release of *All Fall Down*) but to my

Saint and Beatty in a reflective moment.

mind, eye and ear, he neither sounds, looks nor acts like any of them. His is an undeniably individualized and unique persona—but what has been overlooked too often by critics, where Beatty is concerned, is the narrow range of his cinematic effectiveness. In later years Beatty was to get outside that magic, spiritually golden (for him) range. He was no comedian, no multi-faceted personality, no caper-cutter, no universalist of character delineation, and when he got out of his peculiarly limited but kinetically effective persona, he failed.

In *All Fall Down,* Beatty is very much in his element, and very effective. The intense physicality exemplified by his broad shoulders, firm musculature, sturdy trunk, sensual lips, peering small eyes that seem larger than they are because they pinpoint glows of suppressed animalism, are all on effective display in this film. Also, there is that coiled-spring rebellion of spirit that must have often flared up in his confined, repressed, spiritually erosive adolescence, and here his creative imagination can take wing and he can exorcise via the cathartics of art what he could only uncomfortably contain in earlier life amidst frustrating environmental conditions.

Another element gives fire and truth to Beatty's performance in *All Fall Down.* Here he can be the naughty boy of his former adolescent dreams; he can be a devil with the women, conscienceless, a greedy little kid in a sexy candy store; he can work off all the suppressed lusts and physical longings of his repressed Southern Baptist youth. Hence the power of his portrayals in roles conceived, oddly enough, by sensitive male artists of a kind directly antithetical to Beatty's macho image of later years. Thus the infinite irony of Art. Why did it work? Because the "sensitives" instinctively understood the rebellion against suffocating convention, the narcissistic power dreams, the masculine burden and the masculine bond—above all, the narcissistic, sensualized, mirror-principle self-absorption—all of which characterized—and still characterize—Beatty. In later years he was to get off the track artistically only when he went against type, tried to be something he was not, refused to adhere to the integrities and mandates of his narrow but authentic artistic range.

The role of Berry-Berry in *All Fall Down* is in many ways inconceivable without Beatty in the role. He plays a nihilistic, amoral, totally self-absorbed, deeply misogynistic youth, ruled by his grosser passions, coldly selfish, messy in his habits, a slob—but worse, a destructive force.

In the film he is seen through the eyes of his fifteen-year-old brother, Brandon De Wilde, who begins by adoring him unreservedly and ends by despising *and* pitying him. De Wilde is dispatched to Florida with $200 for Beatty which he proceeds to use to bail himself out of jail for assaulting a prostitute. The family thinks it's for him to go into business. With this "business" disposed of, Beatty sends De Wilde home to the family while he signs aboard a yacht to service an older woman who "chicken hawks" virile young men. Other women move in and out of his life; power-driven, narcissistic, unable to contain his endless reserves of sensuality, Berry-Berry, the Beatty character, loves 'em and leaves 'em, builds them up and tears them down with a dizzying change of scene and dame.

His adoring younger brother, once back home, finds life with mom and dad, Angela Lansbury and Karl Malden, humdrum by comparison with what he conceives to be Berry-Berry's "exciting" life. Into their home comes Eva Marie Saint, and De Wilde has a new object to worship.

But Beatty arrives home, Saint succumbs to his animal appeal, gets pregnant by him, is rejected by him, commits suicide, and when De Wilde in outrage goes to kill his brother he finds the woman-killer sobbing like a child. Pity and contempt replace murderous rage in the younger brother's heart, and he leaves Beatty to his fate.

Sterling performances, under the expert, instinctively on-target direction of John Frankenheimer, help make the film. Eva Marie Saint's graceful vulnerability is limned graphically and affectingly; Angela Lansbury's possessive monster of a mother, who has formed the perverse, twisted character of Berry-Berry more than she knows, is a mosaic of shrewdly observed, dinosauric negations. Karl Malden's alcoholic, passive slob of a father is also a shrewd creation. But Beatty, sensual, subtly domineering, dark-spirited, perverse, and in the end childlike in the quicksand morass of his own weaknesses and destructiveness, shown to be as lethal to himself as to others, is the true star of *All Fall Down,* and he deserves to be.

Indeed, so effective is he in this, so much does

*atty's first meeting with Saint at breakfast.
other Angela Lansbury and kid brother Brandon De Wilde look on.*

he profit from Frankenheimer's knowing direction and the insights of the Inge-Herlihy conceptions of character and situation, that when seen in retrospect after seventeen years, *All Fall Down* starkly highlights the waste of Beatty's narrow but authentic talent in a series of blatant miscastings no other star has sustained so consistently.

REVIEWS:

Bosley Crowther in *The New York Times:*
"Everybody in the story is madly in love with a disgusting young man who is virtually a cretin. At least, Warren Beatty plays him so he seems like one. This persistent assumption that everybody should be so blindly devoted to this obnoxious young brute provokes a reasonable spectator

to give up finally in disgust. . . . Surly, sloppy, slow-witted, given to scratching himself, picking his nose, being rude beyond reason to women and muttering about how much he hates the world, this creature that Mr. Beatty gives us is a sad approximation of modern youth . . . Mr. Frankenheimer's direction is conspicuously nervous and harsh, leading one to suspect that he was less demanding of plausibility than of the crushing graphic effect."

Paul V. Beckley in *The New York Herald Tribune:*
"In tone and form [the film] has the air of the autobiographical novel so favored by our writers, the characters sharply defined but considered not so much for themselves as for their effect on the

Problems arise for Beatty and Eva Marie Saint.

narrator, and over everything hangs a tone of disillusionment, the notion that growing up is a sad affair, a post-natal shock. . . . Beatty's performance is the finest of his career. But its very vividness and the exquisite performances of the women he dallies with throw too much interest on the inconsequential and unbalance the whole . . . However, despite this unfortunate feeling of disorientation, the remarkable vigor of the performances almost overcomes it and in the end gives the picture an unmistakable air of reality."

Stanley Kauffmann in *The New Republic:*
"Delicate and moving . . . the dialogue is pithy and nuttily idiomatic, the acting extraordinarily good . . . Warren Beatty, whose two previous film appearances were at best promising, fares much better with the restless, bored Berry-berry. . . . Physically, Beatty has the requisite magnetism; emotionally, he has the coiled-snake tension of black lower-middle-class frustration. What he needs now, as actor, is to develop a more reliable voice, with a wider range."

"Tube" in *Variety:*
"[Beatty] gives his best performance to date, although his range of emotions is not especially wide and his style incorporates distracting elements of Dean and Brando and stresses a kind of monotonous squint-scowl. Still, he has that undeniable star quality."

Baleful matriarch Angela Lansbury watches Beatty and Saint kiss while dad Karl Malden looks on pensively.

Lilith

CAST:
Warren Beatty *(Vincent Bruce)*; Jean Seberg *(Lilith Arthur)*; Peter Fonda *(Stephen Evshevsky)*; Kim Hunter *(Bea Brice)*; Anne Meacham *(Mrs. Yvonne Meaghan)*; James Patterson *(Dr. Lavrier)*; Jessica Walter *(Laura)*; Gene Hackman *(Norman)*; Robert Reilly *(Bob Clayfield)*; Rene Auberjonois *(Howie)*; Lucy Smith *(Vincent's Grandmother)*; Maurice Brenner *(Mr. Gordon)*; Jeanne Barr *(Miss Glassman)*; Richard Higgs *(Mr. Palskis)*; Elizabeth Bader *(Girl at Bar)*; Alice Spivak *(Lonely Girl)*; Walter Arnold *(Lonely*

Advertisement for Lilith

Kim Hunter and Beatty survey the patients.

Girl's Father); Kathleen Phelan *(Lonely Girl's Mother);* Cecilia Ray *(Lilith's Mother in Dream);* Gunnar Peters *(Lilith's Chauffeur in Dream);* L. Jerome Offutt *(Tournament Judge);* Jerome Offutt and Robert Jolivette *(Watermelon Boys);* Dina Paisner *(Psychodrama Moderator);* Pawnee Sills *(Receptionist);* Luther Foulk, Kenneth Fuchs, Steve Dawson, Michael Paras *(Doctors).*

CREDITS:
A Centaur Production. Robert Rossen *(Producer and Director);* Robert Rossen *(Screenplay);* Based on the novel by J.R. Salamanca; Eugen Shuftan *(Photographer);* Avram Avakian *(Editor);* Richard Sylbert *(Production Designer);* Gene Calla-

han *(Set Decorator);* Kenyon Hopkins *(Music Conductor and Composer);* Hugh A. Robertson and Robert Q. Lovett *(Associate Editors);* James Shields and Richard Vorisek *(Sound);* Edward Beyer *(Sound Editor);* Barry Malkin and Lynn Ratener *(Assistant Editors);* Ruth Morley *(Costumes);* Elinor Bunin *(Title Designer);* Jim Di Gangi *(Production Designer);* Eleanor Wolquitt *(Assistant to the Producer);* Larry Sturhahn and Bob Vietro *(Assistant Directors);* Allan Dennis *(Second Assistant Director);* Frederick Jones *(Hairstyles).*

Opened at the New York Film Festival, September 20, 1964. Running time, 114 minutes.

There was to be a gap of some two-and-a-half years between the releases of *All Fall Down* and Beatty's next film, *Lilith.* Since Beatty was twenty-five to twenty-seven years old during this period, and at one of the peaks of his youthful physical appeal, if not of his acting abilities, the time gap is wasteful in retrospect, especially for someone in a line with a premium on youth; someone who at twenty-four had won an estimable screen stardom that many, of any age, sought but few attained.

In recent years Beatty has admitted publicly that in his mid-twenties he was a lazy cuss who enjoyed traveling and having a good time, and that a true sense of responsibility to his talent and his profession came only in the *Bonnie and Clyde* period, when he was touching on thirty.

In any event, the 1962–63 period was a confused one for him. He turned down a number of scripts, raced around Europe, thought and read, made love to whatever lady currently occupied his thoughts, heart and bed. "Unless I can put myself totally into what I am doing, it's just no good," he repeated to whoever would listen. His heart and his total energies had gone into *Splendor, Roman Spring* and even *All Fall Down,* and at the time he stated earnestly (and regretfully) that he knew truly good roles in really fine pictures were few and far between.

When Beatty finally got around to a resumption of filmmaking (he was out of money and reportedly ten thousand dollars in debt) he elected to team up with Robert Rossen, and *Lilith* was the result.

The unwise choice was to prove a filmic low point. He drew almost universally bad reviews. He was later to claim that he and Rossen had not been *simpatico,* that during shooting he had told Rossen they were making a bad picture but Rossen had refused to listen to his ideas on the subject.

"Why should the genius responsible for *All The King's Men* and *The Hustler* have taken account of what a snotty-nosed, wet-behind-the-ears

Beatty tries to decipher the nature of complex patient Jean Seberg.

young vet of three pix had to say anyway?" a Rossen supporter sniffed later. But the results on *Lilith* were to indicate that Beatty's advice, whatever it might have been, coming from a "twenty-seven-year-old snot-nose" or not, could have taken the picture nowhere but up—that is, if anyone's ideas could have.

Both Rossen and Beatty undoubtedly thought they had a classy "art movie" on their hands when they began; their intentions can't be faulted, only their execution. Beatty tended to feel that the bad reviews for his performance were at least partly Rossen's fault. What was equally likely was that he simply didn't identify with his role to any great degree, or if he did, at twenty-seven he lacked the maturity of technique or the perception to articulate whatever he discerned about the character.

And what was *Lilith* about?

Well, it seems that Beatty plays a young war veteran who goes back to his origins in Maryland, and, seeking to be helpful to humanity, applies at a posh mental hospital for the wealthy where he secures a position as an occupational therapist. There he meets beautiful Lilith (Jean Seberg), a patient with the face of an angel and the soul of a devil. She is also demented, in an eerie, gauzy, romantic way, and since Beatty's attention is caught by the angel first and foremost, he falls in love and they begin an affair. But then the horrors start coming out of the proverbial woodwork. Lilith, it seems, is emotionally nymphomaniacal and indiscriminate, choosing her sexual objects without regard to ordinary conventions. She dabbles in lesbianism among other things, wreaks destruction on everyone who falls under her spell, drives lovelorn fellow-inmate Peter Fonda, who is hopelessly enthralled with her, to commit suicide when she rejects his love. Fonda's melodramatic demise hastens Lilith's own terminal slide into all-out madness (it seems she is as vulnerably sensitive as she is unfeelingly ruthless) and Beatty too begins to feel his own connections with reality loosening. He first decides to leave the

Perverse Seberg lights fires in Beatty's heart.

Beatty catches Seberg and fellow patient in compromising situation.

A moody Seberg keeps Beatty on tenterhooks.

hospital's unhealthy atmosphere, but madness is overtaking our hero also, and he shifts from therapist to patient. His own fate seems forbidding at the film's close.

The film was shown at the New York Film Festival to an adverse reaction, and Bosley Crowther cracked that this was the first time a film with all the frou-frou and fussy photography so dear to film festivalites' hearts had failed to make the grade. Eugen Shuftan's photography *is* fussy, overly preoccupied with lambent but inessential nuances and details, and it commits, moreover, the sin of calling too much attention to itself and distracting from the dramatic and acting values, if any. Rossen was not so much out of his depth, perhaps, as out of his element; the darker, more obscure corners of the human heart, the grayish areas between sanity and madness with their many subtle colorations and interpretations were beyond his reach. The J.R. Salamanca novel had probed these odd byways of mind, spirit and heart with masterful literacy. Translated to the screen, and left to the plodding mercies of director Rossen and photographer Shuftan, the doings emerged as

murky, pointless, boring, irritating, when not protractedly excruciating.

Jean Seberg came off best in the acting contingent, closely followed by able supports Anne Meacham and Kim Hunter. Gene Hackman and Rene Auberjonois were also fine in their roles but Beatty won universal disapprobation. *Crowther:* "Mr. Beatty has a sodden way of moving and a monotonous expression that suggests that his character should be getting treatment all through the film. He does not help to clarify matters or generate sympathy." *Crist:* "Beatty is noteworthy for his non-acting and his apparent inability to deliver a line without counting to ten. It's either Super-Method or understandable reluctance, considering the lines." *Variety:* "Beatty cannot surmount the transformations of character to which he is constantly subjected. . . . The audience waits uncomfortably for words which never come while Beatty merely hangs his head or stares into space." *Kauffmann:* "Beatty has only two facets to his acting technique: absolute concentration and understatement to the point of omission. . . . Beatty is all small-scale intensity in an insuffi-

Beatty realizes he is really hooked by the lovely but evil Seberg.

A baffled Beatty contemplates his emotional involvement with the lovely patient.

Beatty socializes with patients Anne Meacham and Peter Fonda.

Horseback riding with Seberg, who has Beatty completely under her spell

Sympathetic doctor Kim Hunter listens to Beatty's outpourings.

A brief moment of playful happiness for Beatty and Seberg

cient voice, so we are never convinced of the transition in him."

Jean Seberg had vastly improved as an actress since her inauspicious debut as Otto Preminger's *St. Joan* in 1956. In the ensuing eight years, especially after her rewarding sojourn among the French film directors, she had developed into an actress of minor, but definite, expressive skills. Whatever honors *Lilith* had to bestow, and they were precious few, went to Miss Seberg, who delineated a complex characterization of a demented girl, half-witch, half-seraph, with subtle delicacy. Some reviewers maintained that the Beatty and Seberg roles cried out for the ministrations of Anthony Perkins and Audrey Hepburn, but in this writer's view, no one could have saved *Lilith*.

Undeterred by his abortive excursion into what he thought was "art," and shrugging it off as a "noble experiment" (while continuing to blame Rossen for not guiding him understandingly through the film's mazes of thought and sensibility), Beatty went from the frying pan of *Lilith* into the fire of *Mickey One,* with Arthur Penn along as director. Again he was to cop out with an abortive "art" attempt.

REVIEWS:
"Whit" in *Variety:*
"Strictly for art house and selected audiences. Its subject is neither pleasant nor conducive to mass entertainment. Columbia Pictures may well be confronted with a problem both in booking and exploiting the subject matter . . . Whatever clar-

ity the narrative has in its early reels is shrouded in mist. Unfoldment is complex and often confusing. Rossen frequently fails to communicate to the spectator. Audience is left in as much of a daze as the hero is throughout most of the film. Warren Beatty undertakes the lead role with a hesitation jarring to the watcher. His dialog generally is restricted to no more than a single, or at most two sentences, and often the audience waits uncomfortably for words which never come while Beatty merely hangs his head or stares into space. The change of character never carries conviction. In adapting the novel, Rossen approaches his task with obvious attempt to shock. Instead, he comes up with something distasteful and, by some standards, offensive. . . . Beatty cannot surmount the transformations of character to which he is constantly subjected."

Bosley Crowther in *The New York Times:*
"A gauzy, opaque work full of clever camera trickery that suggests the eerie, abnormal realms of mental aberration into which the heroine often goes, and loaded with symbolistic details that festival people usually love. Furthermore, in the picture's favor is some vivid structuring of striking images by Mr. Rossen, who is a master at catching the American look of things . . . but Mr. Rossen has not made the eerie, the magical and the baleful blend in any kind of lucid demonstration of what the whole thing means. Is he saying that madness is monstrous or that insanity is good for you? Also, a muddy performance by Warren Beatty doesn't help. Mr. Beatty has a sodden way of moving and a monotonous expression that suggests that his character should be getting treatment all the way through the film. He does not help to clarify matters or generate sympathy."

Judith Crist in *The New York Herald Tribune:*
"It's a muddle of Americana and schizophrenia, sex and sophistry, with a ludicrously lubricious plot and enough fuzzy-wuzzy incoherent camera work to turn it into an unwilling parody on 'art' or 'festival' films at their worst."

Arthur Knight in *The Saturday Review:*
"There is an honest striving for freshness, originality and quality that makes even a relative failure, like *Lilith,* worthy of attention if not unqualified admiration. Clearly the failure of *Lilith* is less in intent than in execution . . . Because of this acute self-consciousness of style, one never really gets very close to the characters; and because the writing and the direction (not to mention Mr. Beatty's performance) seem designed specifically to thwart all identification or empathy, one can only conclude that Mr. Rossen succeeded too well in a misguided attempt at objectivity."

Doctor Kim Hunter realizes Beatty is going mad.

Mickey One

CAST:

Warren Beatty *(Mickey);* Alexandra Stewart *(Jenny);* Hurd Hatfield *(Castle);* Franchot Tone *(Ruby Lapp);* Teddy Hart *(Berson);* Jeff Corey *(Fryer);* Kamatari Fujiwara *(The Artist);* Donne Michelle *(The Girl);* Ralph Foody *(Police Captain);* Norman Gottschalk *(The Evangelist);* Dick Lucas *(Employment Agent);* Benny Dunn *(Nightclub Comic);* Jack Goodman *(Cafeteria Manager);* Jeri Jensen *(Helen);* Charlene Lee *(Singer);* Denise Darnell *(Stripper);* Dick Baker *(Boss at Shaley's);* Helen Witkowski *(Landlady);* William Koza and David Crane *(Art Gallery Patrons);* Mike Fish *(Italian Restaurant Owner);* Greg Louis and Gus Christy *(Bartenders);* David Eisen *(Desk Clerk);* Robert Sickinger *(Policeman);* Lew Prentiss *(Kismet Boss);* Grace Colette *(B-Girl);* Boris Gregurevitch *(Kismet Comic);* Jonas Middleton *(Iggy);* Dink Freeman *(Xanadu M.C.).*

CREDITS:

A Floria-Tatira Production. Arthur Penn *(Producer and Director);* Alan Surgal *(Screenplay);* Eddie Sauter *(Music Composer);* Stan Getz *(Improvisations);* Ghislain Cloquet *(Photographer);* Jack Shaindlin *(Music);* Music conducted by Jack Shaindlin; George Jenkins *(Production Designer);* Aram Avakian *(Editor);* Harrison Starr *(Associate Producer);* Russell Saunders *(Assistant Director);* Domingo Rodriguez *(Costume Designer);* William T. Schneider *(Unit Supervisor);* Lutz Hopke *(Operating Cameraman);* Robert Jiros

...and the name of the game is Mickey!

COLUMBIA PICTURES Presents WARREN BEATTY in Arthur Penn's MICKEY ONE

co-starring HURD HATFIELD · ALEXANDRA STEWART · TEDDY HART · FUJIWARA AND FRANCHOT TONE

Written by aLan surgaL · Produced and Directed by arThur Penn · A FLOrin-TaTira ProDucTion

Trying out the spotlight

(Makeup); Gene Lasko *(Assistant to Producer);* Edward Beyer, Hugh A. Robertson Jr. *(Sound Effects);* Robert Lovett *(Assembly Editor).*

Opened at the Cinema Rendezvous, New York, September 27, 1965, after a screening at the New York Film Festival, September 8, 1965. Running time, 93 minutes.

Mickey One was dubbed by one critic "Kafka out of Al Capone." It elicited a polarized reviewer reaction back in 1965. (Judith Crist loved it, Bos-

ley Crowther hated it, Archer Winsten sided with Crowther, etc.) Regrettably (for it is a well-intentioned, conscientious, Art-for-Art's-Sake-and-Let-the-Boxoffice-Be-Damned effort by people who were sincere) I have to side with Mr. Crowther.

But Warren Beatty, who starred in it, and Arthur Penn, who directed, should get points for one thing: they knew they were making a possible commercial cop-out, and they were frankly aiming at Art with a capital A. That they failed is more a reflection on the defectiveness of their vision and taste and the execution of that vision and taste than on their motivations. They sought to advance the art of the screen (laudable) but lacked the artistic vision and originality to realize their dream (regrettable).

Mickey One functions on two levels: on Level One, Beatty is a nightclub comic who flees Detroit for Chicago because he thinks he is in bad with the mob and is marked for destruction. He bums around in sordid surroundings; works himself into a paranoiac frenzy, sometimes with cause, sometimes not; is befriended by a clear-eyed, sincere girl (Alexandra Stewart) who obviously wishes to help, is aided by agent Teddy Hart in getting bookings in cheap dives, gets auditioned by a better club but runs out; finally, with the girl's help, summons the courage to stop running from the mob and get back into the nightclub spotlight with his routine. On Level Two, we have on our hands a Kafkaesque odyssey of the threat-

eners and the threatened, with Mickey possibly imagining he is persecuted, possibly paranoid-schizophrenic—and then maybe not. On this Level Two, Mickey may be only indulging a nightmare of his own making, carrying the imaginative persecutions of his self-indulgently tortured mind to the ultimate.

Now an artist like Franz Kafka knew what he was saying; he was dealing with the baleful sense of an alien modern universe, hideous in its impersonality, supremely threatening to the lone soul struggling with reality. But the makers of this film were not in Kafka's league when it came to either artistic insights or their proper execution in creatively original terms, and what should be galvanizing and electric, suspenseful, gripping, even mesmerizing, comes through as plodding, contrived and sophomorically pretentious.

Beatty is given any number of opportunities here, but he seems to understand neither his own

Alexandra Stewart consoles a frightened Beatty.

character nor the goings-on any more than the audience does; therefore he comes on surfacey. In his impersonation of a nightclub comic, he falls short of the ready charm, the comic aplomb that is the stock-in-trade of this kind of entertainer; he is strained when he should be spontaneous, and awkward when he should be smoothly professional. It is at times painful to watch him trying to be humorous while pounding on a piano, and when the audience laughs at every weak sally, we are reminded of canned TV laughter, with all its doleful implications.

Nor does he win sympathy for his hunted character, coming across as hysterically confused and psychically disjointed when he should be projecting a mournfully *lost, hunted* quality. The role seems to be beyond the range or understanding of the twenty-eight-year-old Beatty in 1965. It would be interesting to see what a forty-two-year-old 1979-style Beatty could do with this role; the experiences he has sopped up and the insights he has gained might have fleshed out this character more. But it is to Beatty's credit that he tried for what he conceived to be something better, and at a time when commercial considerations would naturally be paramount in most young actors' thoughts.

The picture fancies itself Dostoievskian as well as Kafkaesque—and the supporting characters are on occasion hideous as gargoyles and just as unappetizing. As the agent, Teddy Hart is a horrible gnomelike image that symbolizes—what? Franchot Tone, sixty-one when he made this, comes across wizened, masklike, almost mummi-

Hurd Hatfield gives Beatty the broken bottle treatment.

fied, with bright, manic eyes staring out of an immobile, pasty face.

Hurd Hatfield, twenty years older than when he was the beau-homme-sans-merci protagonist of *The Picture of Dorian Gray,* is obviously gotten up to exemplify Dorian two decades later, had he become a nightclub entrepreneur and front man for the mob. Wildean implications are underlined even further with Beatty roughly pushing Hatfield's encroaching hand from his arm; there are hints that Hatfield is playing an aging gay who lusts after Beatty, but since the film was made in 1965, this is not stressed unduly. It does raise the interesting point about Beatty, though, that has cropped up regarding his performances over the years—that he comes across in some incarnations as neither homosexual nor heterosexual, but rather as narcissist supreme. For Beatty seems to *enjoy* Hatfield's silky addressals while roughly rebuffing them.

Jeff Corey is a fine actor with a solid, manly projection, and he seems the only human being, Miss Stewart excepted, in the cast; he projects tough decisiveness without unwholesome menace, so may possibly have been miscast. Had the movie been made now, something more interesting might have been made of Hatfield's effete character, but even in 1965 terms this is one point that does get across.

Columbia Pictures reportedly went along with Beatty's and Penn's "art" experiment because they were 1) tired of arguing against it, 2) recalled that Beatty and Penn had been box-office winners on occasion in the past, 3) the budget was less than a million dollars.

Penn gives it the college try with various touches: autos, possibly with dead gang victims inside, crushed into steel oblongs by giant machines; dark, forbidding streets with leering, ugly faces shoved into the eye of the camera; the neon-

Beatty cogitates behind a door.

lit hell of city streets surveyed intimately. But the action is so stylized as to be dehumanized, cold, remote, mechanical. It is strangely disjointed, nervous, pretentious. Occasionally there are sharply-observed small vignettes of people with interesting faces.

To this day, Beatty defends *Mickey One,* and considers it a worthy artistic effort, a sincere attempt to stretch the esthetic possibilities of the screen. The film failed commercially, but has generated much pro-and-con discussion.

REVIEWS:
Judith Crist in *The New York Herald Tribune:*
"A brilliant original screen work, visually exciting and intellectually satisfying, a credit to everyone involved . . . this very contemporary film, dealing in allegorical terms with the burgeoning terrors of our time, introduces us to some fresh

and deeply impressive talents, talents that blend into the cooperative artistry that is moviemaking at its best. Plot and dialogue, performance and score communicate in aural and visual terms a story on two levels that throbs with immediacy on both. . . . Warren Beatty, so long over-mannered and under-revealed, emerges brilliantly as the Mickey who is "guilty of not being innocent," smooth and fast on the routines, suddenly a quivering lump of terror, furtive-eyed, without trust or hope until he finally admits that he hasn't the guts to keep running scared . . . Mr. Penn has used Resnais-like techniques in probing memory and experience, in alternating between past and present, repeating the scene, the remark, the mood that has significance. Thus he transcends the literal and in true cinematic style rounds out the story by suggestion, by abandoning chronology, by restoring to total experience."

Saying it with music to Alexandra Stewart

Bumming around in Chicago

Archer Winsten in *The New York Post:*
"A film as modern, garish and hectic as neon. Director Arthur Penn has decided in advance that this was going to be one for the audience that wants to think and grapple with modern art. Star Warren Beatty was willing to gamble with this kind of thing rather than go for the sure buck. Columbia Pictures, quaking in its financial boots, was persuaded to go along with these two . . . call it the chromium-plated, neon-lighted surface of modern life, the stress that drives modern man to his head-shrinkers. Or call it a clever movie-maker's manipulation of these standard elements of this known art condition . . . The picture's fundamental flaw is the key figure, Mickey, as played by Warren Beatty. Beatty gives it the fast-chatter routine which he seems to have learned for the occasion, but it doesn't come out of him with authority. For instance, he's not up to the style of the minor burlesque hall comic who has a bit. He's not in total control of the rest of his character either because that's not his kind of character. It can't fool anyone who believed him in his good ones like *All Fall Down* and *Splendor in the Grass.* This is all a surface act, surface sweat. It's not inside him because he doesn't understand it. You get tired of [the film] because you don't really give a damn unless you happen to be living a similar sweat-out yourself, or think you are, or are willing to imagine that other people are like this. In other words, if you want to be with this picture, you have to supply a very large share of its insides, basing them on these brilliant, very considerable outsides. These things being so, there should be an unusually wide diversity of critical opinion. This department votes

At an arcade he wonders about his luck.

Beatty on the lam

no, with regret, for the effort is all-out and it is not flawed with commercial considerations."

Bosley Crowther in *The New York Times:*
"Whether this lurid demonstration is intended to represent what goes on in the psyche of the hero as he runs through his grim experiences, or is meant to be a sort of symbolical allegory of the agony of life for those who can't face 'the big crap game' is not made clear. This is most confusing and annoying—a dangerous weakness in the structure of the film. . . . Also, Mr. Beatty is affected and oddly amateurish in the way he presents the emotional torments and startled reactions of his heel. Shapeless and superficial, his chap generates little sense of real psychological disturbance with which one can have empathy . . . The picture is interesting mainly for the elaborate photographics of Mr. Penn—his delight in using his camera to scan the phantasmagoria of city life, or to view a superfluously staged happening such as one of those pyrotechnical things done by the pop artist, Jean Tinguely."

Promise Her Anything

CAST:
Warren Beatty *(Harley Rummel);* Leslie Caron *(Michele O'Brien);* Bob Cummings *(Dr. Peter Brock);* Hermione Gingold *(Mrs. Luce);* Lionel Stander *(Sam);* Asa Maynor *(Rusty);* Keenan Wynn *(Ange);* Cathleen Nesbitt *(Dr. Brock's Mother);* Michael Bradley *(John Thomas);* Bessie Love *(Woman in Pet Shop);* Riggs O'Hara *(Glue Sniffer);* Mavis Villiers *(Middle-aged Woman);* Hal Galili *(First Moving Man);* Warren Mitchell, Sydney Taffler *(Panelists);* Ferdy Mayne *(Fettucini);* Margaret Nolan *(Stripper);* Vivienne Ven-

Beatty in a tender moment with Leslie Caron

tura *(Third Stripper);* Anita Sharp Bolster *(Baby Sitter);* George Moon *(Dancer);* Charlotte Holland *(Dancer's Wife);* Chuck Julian *(Grocery Clerk);* Michael Chaplin *(Beatnik).*

CREDITS:
A Ray Stark–Seven Arts Presentation; Stanley Rubin *(Producer);* Arthur Hiller *(Director);* William Peter Blatty *(Screenplay);* Based on a story by Arne Sultan and Marvin Worth; Douglas Slocombe *(Photographer);* Lynn Murray *(Music);* Title song by Burt Bacharach and Hal David, sung by Tom Jones; Wilfrid Shingleton *(Art Director);* David Ffolkes *(Set Decorator);* John Shirley *(Editor);* George Stephenson *(Sound);* Beatrice Dawson *(Costumes);* Bob Lawrence *(Makeup);* Charles Parker *(Miss Caron's Makeup);* Pat McDermott *(Hairstyles);* Jack Smith *(Production Executive);* Jack Smith *(Production Manager);* Ronnie Bear *(Assistant Director);* Ted Sturgis *(Assistant Director);* Color by Technicolor.

Opened at the DeMille and Beekman Theatres, New York, February 22, 1966. Running time, 98 minutes.

In a rather blatant *and* tasteless—attempt to cash in on, or maybe just satisfy, public interest in Beatty's affair with Leslie Caron, whose husband, English director Peter Hall, named Beatty co-respondent in a messy 1965 British divorce suit, some folk got the not-so-bright idea of casting Beatty and Caron in a frothy comedy with some naughty sex angles (naughty by 1966 standards, perhaps; banal and emasculated in 1979). After his two disastrous experiences with cinematic "art" in America, Beatty decided he needed a change of pace, so went to England after assorted travelings and millings-around, and, with Miss Caron, did the frothy, foolish confection called *Promise Her Anything.*

Even the title had tastelessly leering implications, given the current Beatty–Caron involvement, to say nothing of all the other women in his past—and the doings themselves reflected no credit on the sometimes creatively sincere director Arthur Hiller or on Beatty and Caron.

In this rampant farce, Beatty went in for his latest self-delusion: that he was a comedian of skills so formidable as to have surpassed Cary Grant in his prime. Delusion it was, for Beatty as a farceur showed himself as awkward, fumbling and heavy-handed in imparting genuine comic feel to a film as the English settings were in suggesting Greenwich Village, where the story was set. Neither the buildings, shrubbery, accents, streets, walls, children nor anything else looked like any Greenwich Village we ever knew, and some good actors were woefully wasted, including Bob Cummings, an experienced and adept farceur who should have had Beatty's role; Cathleen Nesbitt, a distinguished English actress of impeccable taste and histrionic flair who was given jive talk to enunciate (as a joke it fell flat); Lionel Stander, who had grown hoary but was thought to be horny, pawing at a redhead; and assorted splendid English actors whose one fault was that they didn't talk Greenwich-ese or even American-ese with true conviction, thus adding to the ersatz inanities of the piece.

William Peter Blatty, who had done *John Goldfarb, Please Come Home,* sank to new lows of ponderous *unfunniness* with *Promise Her Anything.* The doings proved tedious, old-hat, literal, heavy and most depressing at moments meant to be most comic. The story we will pass over quickly: Caron is a widow who moves into a Greenwich Village apartment with her infant son, Michael Bradley. Upstairs lives dapper Beatty, who wants to make art movies but instead does burlesque fare to keep alive (an autobiographical tinge here?). Beatty likes Caron, indeed comes to love her, but Caron wants child psychologist Cummings, who really hates kids. Cummings is her boss, but she keeps her infant secret from him to improve her cap-setting chances. Among the subsequent inanities: Beatty uses the kid in his sex movies; the baby winds up in Cummings' clinic where Beatty makes a burlesque film in the kid's hospital room for reasons that make no sense at all. Cummings has a hidden camera in the room to record Baby's behavior so Beatty's malfeasances are discovered. An infuriated Caron wants no more of suitor Beatty but when he saves Baby from a crane outside her window, it is apparent he is to be Number One Man.

Nudie pix, child psychology and a host of other then-current crazes are the objects of would-be satirical thrusts, all of which fail to hit home. The baby steals most of the show, dominating the film's first half hour; many reviewers opined he should have been handed the whole thing. Nudie

Caron finds that Beatty's attempted fathering of Michael Bradley is less than a success.

setups, spoofs on sex, a host of comic dalliances are tried and found wanting, and Bob Cummings, who with Cathleen Nesbitt and Lionel Stander (in the right role) were the sole people aboard with a true professional feel for comic nuance, are given little chance to bail out anyone or anything. Miss Nesbitt makes the most of her sharp lines, Cummings does what he can with a role that is more passive than catalytic, and Bessie Love gets about two lines to say. After seeing the picture she was probably relieved she didn't get to share more fully in its affectations.

There is a lot of tricky, fustian editing, 1966-style, with stop-motion gimmicks and experiments with Technicolor that don't always take. Beatty co-stars the baby with a sexy redhead in a revealing bikini but the kid obviously prefers his red building blocks. One critic, striving to be kindly no matter what the cost, wound up his review with: "Say this for the London Studios' Greenwich Village. It may not be cluttered with Beatniks, but at least it looks sanitary. As for gurgling Master Bradley, what a trouper! Promise him anything."

Beatty as Cary Grant was obviously not a howling success. Beatty took the hint, and comedy of a cutesy-poo variety, the kind that cried out for a fey Grant–Stewart–Niven touch beyond the Beatty range and powers, went off his list for the foreseeable future.

Psychologist Bob Cummings wants to know what goes on with fiancee Caron and Beatty.

REVIEWS:

Howard Thompson in *The New York Times:*
"Good-natured bounce the picture has, but the going gets mighty bumpy and frantic in this harmless story. . . . Under the game direction of Arthur Hiller, the first half percolates nicely indeed . . . the picture has obvious but palatable zing, until it gets out of hand. Most of the seams show blatantly, in the slapdash finale that has Mr. Beatty, who is otherwise quite deft, swinging wildly on a runaway construction crane with the baby perched on top. Say this for the London Studios' Greenwich Village. It may not be cluttered with beatniks, but at least it looks sanitary. As for gurgling Master Bradley, what a trouper! Promise him anything, even *Hamlet.*"

Judith Crist in *The New York Herald Tribune:*
"Greenwich Village was never like this . . . Miss Caron is the widow; her French accent garbles a lot of her lines and that is good. Mr. Beatty is the dirty movie-maker; he says his lines straight and that is bad. Robert Cummings is the psychologist; he says his lines and that is sad . . . *Promise Her Anything* succeeds on several levels, each a low one, in proving that neither gifted professionals nor eighteen-month-old babies can rise above some material."

Time:
"Shortly after splashing headlines last year as off-screen lovers in an unsavory divorce action, Leslie Caron and Warren Beatty pooled their talents in a sex farce. Surprisingly enough, it is an amiable, entertaining fiction and nowhere near so scandalous as life itself . . . Leslie oozes genuine charm, and Beatty, in his first light comedy role, shows an unexpected flair for foolishness."

Beatty confronts Keenan Wynn at an inopportune moment.

Jumping to the rescue when tot Michael Bradley gets caught on a moving crane

Grateful mother Caron begins to seriously consider her child's rescuer as a marriage candidate.

"Murf" in *Variety:*

"A light, refreshing comedy-romance set in Greenwich Village but filmed in England, which satirizes both child psychology and nudie pix in a tasteful, effective manner. Well-paced direction of many fine performances, generally sharp scripting and other good production elements add up to a satisfying comedy for most audiences . . . director Arthur Hiller has overcome a basic problem; specifically, that Leslie Caron and Warren Beatty are not known as film comics. His fine solution has been to spotlight baby Michael Bradley in the first thirty minutes, when Miss Caron is establishing an easy audience rapport, while Beatty slides into a likeable groove via energetic tumbles and other manifestations of youthful enthusiasm."

All's well and happy as Beatty and Caron decide life can be good—together.

Kaleidoscope

CAST:

Warren Beatty *(Barney Lincoln)*; Susannah York *(Angel McGinnis)*; Clive Revill *(Inspector "Manny" McGinnis)*; Eric Porter *(Harry Dominion)*; Murray Melvin *(Aimes)*; George Sewell *(Billy)*; Stanley Meadows *(Dominion Captain)*; John Junkin *(Dominion Porter)*; Larry Taylor *(Dominion Chauffeur)*; Yootha Joyce *(Museum Receptionist)*; Jane Birkin *(Exquisite Thing)*; George Murcell *(Johnny)*; Anthony Newlands *(Leeds)*.

Advertising copy for Kaleidoscope.

Susannah York and Beatty find a moment of happiness.

CREDITS:
A Winkast Production. Presented by Jerry Gershner and Elliott Kastner; Elliott Kastner *(Producer)*; Jack Smight *(Director)*; Robert and Jane-Howard Carrington *(Screenplay)*; from an original story by the Carringtons; Christopher Challis *(Photography)*; Stanley Myers *(Music Composer and Conductor)*; John Jympson *(Editor)*; Maurice Carter *(Art Director)*; David Ffolkes *(Set Decorator)*; Rusty Coppleman *(Sound)*; Dudley Messenger and Gordon K. McCallum *(Sound Associates)*; Maurice Binder *(Titles)*; Sally Tuffin and Marion Foale *(Miss York's Costumes)*; Peter Medak *(Associate Producer)*; Denis Holt *(Production Supervisor)*; Marion Rosenberg *(Assitant to the Producer)*; Kip Gowans *(Assistant Director)*. Color by Technicolor.

Opened at Radio City Music Hall, September 22, 1966. Running time, 103 minutes.

Beatty taking his ease on a bed with Susannah York

Confronted by mid-1966 with his failure at art and his failure at comedy, a confused and non-plussed — and maybe punch-drunk — Beatty decided that all that remained cinematically to be conquered — or more accurately, attempted — was the kind of fast-paced, kaleidoscopic "caper" stuff then so much in vogue. And that is all that *Kaleidoscope* is — a caper with lots of scenery change, tricky photography, garish Technicolor, forced comedy that more often than not falls flat, and downright amateurish performances from Beatty and Susannah York. Their ineptitudes are all the more stark, surrounded as they are by excellent actors like Clive Revill and Eric Porter.

This was Beatty's second British film in 1966, this time for Warners release, and it was shot in London and on the French Riviera. On hand to guide the action this time was Jack Smight, who had given a good account of himself as director of Paul Newman's *Harper*.

The story was one of those convoluted things so dear to "caper" fans, with Beatty busily dashing back and forth, making mischief wherever the spirit moves him, and in the final half hour running seriously afoul of villains who really mean their malfeasances.

The story is tediously labyrinthine but we'll try to cover it quickly and clearly: Beatty is a wealthy American, a playboy, dilettante and thrill-seeker, who takes up briefly in London with mod dress designer Susannah York. Then it's off to Geneva where he breaks into a playing card factory and etches secret marks on cards destined for leading European gambling casinos. At Monte

A light moment on the stairs with Susannah York

Carlo he makes a fortune with the "fixed" cards, tours other casinos with an ever more suspicious York, who finally blabs to Daddy (Clive Revill), who of course is a Scotland Yard man. He nabs Beatty but promises to let him off if he will assist in capturing Eric Porter, an infamous narcotics smuggler. Porter likes poker and Beatty lures him into a game and wins consistently, even with unmarked cards. Porter then lures Beatty to his estate, using York as bait, and gets back his cash by force. The young couple, trying to escape, are almost killed by the gang but are saved just in the nick of time by Daddy's Scotland Yard men.

Had all this been told with some wit, style, literacy and a correct blend of writing, directorial and photographic skills, *Kaleidoscope* might have been a smash sleeper of the kind Beatty desperately needed, what with three bad pictures in a row behind him. But it was not to be. Trouble for Beatty, cinematically, seemed to run not just in threes, but in fours. "Both foolish and frustrating —Smight substitutes clutter for style. . . . uncannily laughless . . . Warren Beatty, all-American card-sharp, proves again, as he did in *Promise Her Anything,* that fey comedy is not his forte" (Judith Crist). *Time,* more gentle, reported: "*Kaleidoscope* succeeds with a dash that often disguises the balderdash," but added, "Hero Warren Beatty tries so hard to act like Sean Connery that once or twice he almost develops a line in his face." Crowther of the *Times,* rarely a friend of Beatty in print (he was *really* to give it to him in the much-ballyhooed *Bonnie and Clyde* the following year) intoned: "Both young people are forced and flat, fumbling like a couple of dressed-up amateurs in an environment of professional chic. As a consequence, the hyperbolic clowning of Clive Revill and the villainous pretending of Eric Porter are thrown out of comedy balance, and the symmetry of design is lost." Crowther applied a parting coup de grace to *Kaleidoscope* with the words: "What we're left with is an end-

Beatty breaking into the card factory

Admirers kibitz while Beatty starts to break the bank

less rotation of splattered, absurd activity within an eye-filling succession of colorful indoor and outdoor sets."

A four-time loser in his unceasing search for "winning" material for the screen and his by-now-battered stellar image, Beatty thought long and hard about his next film. He had sacrificed his all for so-called art, but his conceptions of art had somehow failed him. He had seen the fruitlessness of being the new Cary Grant; such specialized talents were simply not up his alley. Caper films were a better bet, he reasoned, but only if they were done well, with a special panache that was as much luck, a magic combination of ingredients, as it was design and calculated expertise.

He knew that his chances were running out. The next time out, no matter what, he could not afford to fail. Five-time-losers were losers in spades; now it was up to him to come up with a winning Ace.

REVIEWS:
Time:
"The robbery sequence is just about the trickiest bit of flim-flam since the jewel job in *Topkapi*. Unhappily, the trickiness is not confined to one episode; this picture skillfully but all too shamelessly mimics the gimmicks that have transformed the Fleming formula into the Bond bind. Nevertheless, if the success of a thriller can be measured in thrills, *Kaleidoscope* succeeds with a dash that often disguises the balderdash . . . Hero Warren Beatty tries so hard to act like Sean Connery that once or twice he almost develops a line in his face . . . As for the continuity, it goes thun-

Susannah York surveys Beatty's gaming prowess.

Marking the cards at the factory

derballing along from zoom shot to crash cut to color-diller costume sequence till the spectator's senses are knocked eight ways to Sunday. Not a profound experience but an extravagantly stimulating one. At times, indeed, the moviegoer may wonder if he isn't looking at *Kaleidoscope* through a kaleidoscope."

"Murf" in *Variety:*
"The production has some eyecatching mod clothing styles, inventive direction and other values which sustain the simple story line . . . entertaining comedy suspenser . . . the related progress of the story becomes, under Jack Smight's direction, more dynamic through the use of Christopher Challis's mobile Technicolor camera. Subsidiary

events and characterizations keep the pace moving. Final half-hour is all serious drama. All performances are okay . . . Overall, this modest little picture could prove a sleeper."

Bosley Crowther in *The New York Times:*
"This go at romantic comedy is a constant succession of busy and colorful pictorial scenes that are almost as empty of narrative substance as those pretty designs in a kaleidoscope. To be sure, there is a sort of story in it. But it is [full] of many deliberate implausibilities . . . the conception and playing of the characters are just as frivolous. Warren Beatty is made to be a cool, casual, flippant gentleman gambler who cheats mainly pour le sport, and Susannah York is made an odd-mod

A location shot with Susannah York on London's famed Carnaby Street

dress-designer with the airiness of a bird. And in direction of these people, Jack Smight has tried to have them get the nonchalance and glitter of purely fictional sophistication. But alas, they do not get it. Both young people are forced and flat, fumbling like a couple of dressed-up amateurs in an environment of professional chic. . . . What we're left with is an endless rotation of splattered, absurd activity within an eyefilling succession of colorful indoor and outdoor sets."

Judith Crist in *The New York World Journal-Tribune:*
"A romantic comedy adventure film can get by at very least by virtue of its plot or its style and succeeds, of course, by a combination of both. Alas, [this] story is both foolish and frustrating, and director Jack Smight, so impressive in his recent *Harper,* substitutes clutter for style in his handling thereof . . . there's something uncannily laughless about this film. Warren Beatty, all-American card-sharp, proves again, as he did in *Promise Her Anything,* that fey comedy is not his forte . . . we clatter from one flat piece of improvisation to another. It's all pretty and pointless with limited entertainment for all. An apt name indeed, *Kaleidoscope.*"

Bonnie and Clyde

CAST:

Warren Beatty *(Clyde Barrow)*; Faye Dunaway *(Bonnie Parker)*; Michael J. Pollard *(C.W. Moss)*; Gene Hackman *(Buck Barrow)*; Estelle Parsons *(Blanche)*; Denver Pyle *(Sheriff Frank Hamer)*; Dub Taylor *(Ivan Moss)*; Evans Evans *(Velma Davis)*; Gene Wilder *(Eugene Grizzard)*; James Stiver *(Grocery Store Owner)*.

CREDITS:

A Tatira-Hiller Production; Warren Beatty *(Producer)*; Arthur Penn *(Director)*; David Newman and Robert Benton *(Screenplay)*; Burnett Guffey *(Photography)*; Charles Strouse *(Music)*; Dean Tavoularis *(Art Director)*; Raymond Paul *(Set Decorations)*; Dede Allen *(Editor)*; Danny Lee *(Special Effects)*; Francis E. Stahl *(Sound)*; Robert

Warren Beatty makes with the double draw.

Towne *(Special Consultant);* Theodora Van Runkle *(Costumes);* Robert Jiras *(Makeup);* Gladys Witten *(Hairstyles);* Russ Saunders *(Production Manager);* Elaine Michael *(Assistant to the Producer);* Jack N. Reddish *(Assistant Director).* Color by Technicolor.

Opened August 13, 1967, at the Forum and Murray Hill Theatres, New York. Running time, 111 minutes.

For *Bonnie and Clyde,* Beatty won an Academy Award nomination for the year 1967 (he lost to Rod Steiger's fine performance in *In the Heat of the Night).* Critics were, as usual, divided as to the merits of his performance and the quality of the film that emerged, but they did give Beatty an "A" for courage, persistence and guts. Failure had come to seem the most heinous of sins to Beatty by this point, and he was determined that his *Bonnie and Clyde* project was going to be a success no matter what.

Beatty and Dunaway stage one of their bank heists.

Dunaway hoists the shootin' iron while Beatty feints.

Pollard, Beatty, Hackman and Dunaway (right) force Sheriff Denver Pyle to pose with them.

When he brought his package — story, stars, director — to Warner Bros., he shrewdly and far-sightedly demanded a rising-percentage-scale against possible grosses. Since no one at Warners in 1967 remotely believed — or even conceived — that *Bonnie and Clyde* was going to turn into the bonanza that it did, with profits in the tens of millions, their attitude toward Beatty and his projected deal was essentially: "Sure, sure, give him what he asks for. If we get back our negative cost, we'll count ourselves lucky, and he'll wind up getting thirty percent or whatever it is of *nothing.*"

The surprise result got Beatty, at thirty, a fresh lease on life in a Hollywood where success alone elicited any true respect and a star was judged only by the box-office proceeds of his last film. The individualism and integrity that Beatty had sincerely espoused at twenty-five, as indicated in his interviews at the time, had changed to a pragmatic success orientation. Tired of so-so pictures, he had decided to "go Hollywood" and prove he could play the Hollywood game as well as any of them.

Beatty's allies and assorted apologists have been at pains to point out that the economic side of the business had grown increasingly important, not to say crucial, by the mid-1960s, what with production costs rising each year, and cited him as a martyr to such "art" experiments as *Lilith* and *Mickey One.*

After all, they stressed, Beatty was a practical, level-headed, realistic young man and the time had come to follow the "if you can't lick 'em join 'em" philosophy. But others who also admired Beatty expressed sadness that in the pursuit of commercially viable properties he had not been able to come up with characterizations that properly highlighted his limited but authentic artistry, as the roles in his first three films had done for him.

The story of Clyde Barrow and Bonnie Parker had been covered, in whole or in part, in a number of prior films, for instance in *The Bonnie Parker Story* (1958) with Dorothy Provine as Bonnie and Jack Hogan as Clyde. Directed by one William Witney and produced by one Stanley Shpetner (*sic*), it came and went soon enough.

The plot? Who doesn't know by now about the impotent Clyde, who reportedly was also a prison homosexual, and the thrill-seeking Bonnie, robbing the rich to give to the poor (or so they liked to maintain), meanwhile leaving a trail of blood in bank robberies and assorted depredations-de-luxe from Iowa to Texas in the years 1933 and 1934. Much was made of their being "products of their time," but the obvious answer to such muddled philosophizing is: what about all the good, decent people of that period who survived quietly and respectably, suffering through social and economic upheavals without cutting-up or running-wild in the lurid Barrow–Parker manner. Of course the great unsung, unnoted, unsensational souls of that period were not pathological, or irredeemably character-flawed, hence missed notoriety — a notoriety that some call fame. Evil is always more attention-getting, more striking, more vivid than good, and that has become by now the hoariest of clichés (though clichés, to *become* clichés, imply a great deal of strength and truth in their underlying insights).

The two negative reviews of the film by Bosley Crowther of *The New York Times* (one for the Montreal Film Festival opening, and one for his regular critic's pillar) unleashed a hot pro-and-con debate, with the more indecisive reviewers shifting initially unfavorable reviews to more muted recants (such as some of them were to do, for unexplained reasons, four years later in the case of another Beatty film, *McCabe & Mrs. Miller).* Indeed, *The New York Times* printed during 1967–68 a number of pro-and-con observations on *Bonnie,* Crowther offered additional observations after that, *Variety* covered the brouhaha with two full pages, and for a whole year a journalistic tempest was generated.

Soon director Arthur Penn got into the act with an interview in which he stated, rather equivocally: "Some people may be stimulated by violence but some people are also turned on by music." He then added obscurantism to equivocation by adding, "The important question is whether the work itself is good or bad art. I suppose violence can seem isolated and arbitary, but even so, you can't 'censor' bad art."

Beatty's star charisma and potent chemistry were as evident as ever in the handsomely photographed (however gory) color film, but he did seem unsuited to the role of Barrow. He seemed to lack the complexity of the original's character makeup, the wild passion often unleashed, the sexual-ambivalence projections, and the patho-

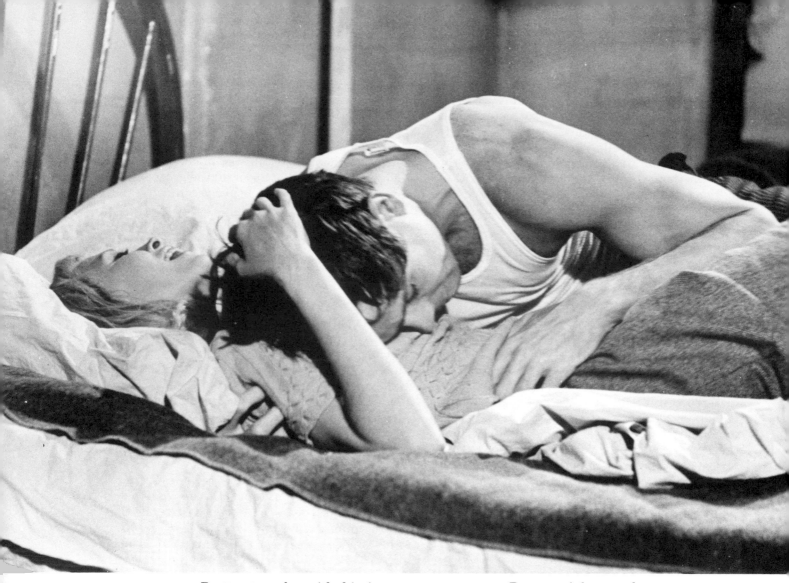

Beatty struggles with his impotence to assuage Dunaway's love needs.

Beatty shoots it out at a garage door.

logical but single-minded purpose that motivated Barrow. Faye Dunaway, though somewhat too ladylike and actressy for the Bonnie role, got herself across vividly in spots, and Michael J. Pollard, Gene Hackman and Estelle Parsons were effective as the pal, brother and sister-in-law respectively.

One wag nailed Beatty's part succinctly: "From splendoring in the grass to wallowing in the gore —and green."

REVIEWS:
Judith Crist in *Vogue:*
"With *Bonnie and Clyde,* Warren Beatty and Arthur Penn firmly establish themselves as one of the most excitingly creative teams in American moviemaking . . . where the fact ends and the fiction begins is no longer decipherable or very relevant to the brief history of the couple who posthumously won folk-hero status. What is relevant is that they were drifters, nobodies, yearning to be any kind of somebodies, rebels with no cause beyond the moment's rebellion. They hap-pened at a time when a third of the nation was rootless but immobilized by the Depression, debilitated and apathetic, and ready to admire in secret the surface derring-do of those who could get away with striking at the Establishment. . . . It is in retrospect that the pathos of this pair, so much a product of their time and so potentially to be paralleled in ours, is evident—and this evidence provides the particular distinction of what might well have been just another gangster movie, another glorification of violence and rebellion, another bit of lip-service to morality . . . Warren Beatty, so often merely a promising performer, fulfills himself as Clyde, revealing every inward weakness and outward ferocity of the man for whom weapons and the driver's wheel provide potency. . . . Naturalism—in characters and background—is the mark of this film in its technical perfections. Saturated in time and place, we are left with the universality of the theme and its particular contemporary relevance. And this is the triumph of *Bonnie and Clyde.*"

Pollard, Hackman, Beatty and Dunaway beat it out of the bank with their swag

Pollard, Hackman and Beatty rough up Sheriff Denver Pyle while Estelle Parsons kibitzes.

Beatty and Dunaway hold off the cops.

Dunaway goes to aid of wounded Beatty.

Films in Review:
"*Bonnie and Clyde* is so incompetently written, acted, directed and produced it would not be worth noticing were a claque not attempting to promote the idea that its sociopathology is art . . . the script [is] dementia praecox of the most pointless sort. That is, it endeavors to do simultaneously such antithetical things as: 1) "explain" the Barrow gang of real-life punks who killed eighteen people in the course of Texas-Oklahoma hold-ups in the Depression days of the '30s; *kid* these real-life hold-ups and murders via slap-stick (very amateurishly); 3) deploy male impotence (Clyde's) throughout the film as an *aphrodisiac for pathics of both sexes;* 4) wallow in sado-masochism (the camera dwells on an eye as it is shot from its socket, on a head that is blown apart); 5) arouse sympathy for Clyde Barrow and Bonnie Parker when the police ultimately ambush them and shoot them down. Who is the producer of so adolescently ignorant a film? Warren Beatty, who also plays Clyde, and, in doing so, adds his own ignorances to the character-inconsistencies of the script. Who directed? Arthur

Dunaway and Beatty in a relatively quiet moment.

Penn, whose artistic integrity is about on the level of Beatty's acting ability — i.e., close to zero. . . . There is *evil* in the *tone* of the writing, acting and direction of this film, the calculated effect of which is to incite in the young the delusion that armed robbery and murder are mere 'happenings.'"

Time:
"A strange and purposeless mingling of fact and claptrap that teeters uneasily on the brink of burlesque. Like Bonnie and Clyde themselves, the film rides off in all directions and ends up full of holes. Beatty, playing the lead, does a capable job, within the limits of his familiar, insolent, couldn't-care-less manner, of making Barrow the amiable varmint he thought himself to be . . . the

real fault with *Bonnie and Clyde* is its sheer, tasteless aimlessness . . . Repeated bursts of Country-style music punctuating the bandits' grisly ventures, and a sentimental interlude with Bonnie's old Maw photographed through a hazy filter, aim at irony and miss by a mile."

Variety:
"Incongruously couples comedy with crime . . . Conceptually, the film leaves much to be desired, because killings and the backdrop of the Depression are scarcely material for a bundle of laughs. However, the film does have some standout interludes. . . . Inconsistency of direction is the most serious fault of *Bonnie and Clyde,* which has some good ingredients, although they are not meshed together well . . . like the film itself, the

Gene Hackman and Beatty clown.

performances are mostly erratic. Beatty is believable at times, but his characterization lacks any consistency."

Hollis Alpert in *The Saturday Review:*
"Filmically, it represents a high point in the directional work of Arthur Penn; it is exceedingly well made; it has an astonishingly good performance by Warren Beatty, captures fairly accurately a sense of the period, and attempts to understand the two natures of the young man and his girl, Bonnie Parker. . . . What is bothersome about the picture is that the writers aren't able to make clear their own attitudes toward the two criminals . . . the film is unusual, and even fascinating, in its depiction of the reactions to the crime wave by people who had no reason to love banks, and of the sheer seeming normality of the way of life of the criminals. But will the picture do well because of its more probing aspects, or because of the vivid violence with which it is filled? Warner Brothers, I am sure, knows the answer."

Bosley Crowther in *The New York Times:*
"It is a cheap piece of baldfaced slapstick comedy that treats the hideous depredations of that sleazy, moronic pair as though they were as full of fun and frolic as the jazz-age cut-ups in *Thoroughly Modern Millie* . . . this blending of farce with brutal killings is as pointless as it is lacking in taste, since it makes no valid commentary on the already travestied truth. And it leaves an astonished critic wondering just what purpose Mr. Penn and Mr. Beatty think they serve with this strangely antique, sentimental claptrap."

Dunaway and Beatty attempt to consummate their love.

The Only Game in Town

CAST:
Elizabeth Taylor *(Fran)*; Warren Beatty *(Joc Grady)*; Charles Braswell *(Lockwood)*; Hank Henry *(Tony)*.

CREDITS:
A George Stevens–Fred Kohlmar Production; Fred Kohlmar *(Producer)*; George Stevens *(Director)*; Frank D. Gilroy *(Screenplay)*; Based on a

Taylor and Beatty realize they are deeply in love.

Taylor deplores Beatty's gambling fever.

play by Frank D. Gilroy; Maurice Jarre *(Music)*; Mia Fonssagrives and Vicki Tiel *(Costumes)*; Henri Decae *(Photographer)*; Herman Blumenthal and Auguste Capelier *(Art Directors)*; Walter M. Scott and Jerry Wunderlich *(Set Decorators)*; L.B. Abbott, A.S.C. and Art Cruikshank *(Special Photographic Effects)*; John W. Holmes, William Sands and Pat Shade *(Editors)*; Christian Ferry *(Unit Production Manager)*; Robert Swink *(Second Unit Director)*; Robert Doudell *(Assistant Director)*; Jo de Bretagne and David Dockendorf *(Sound)*; Michel Menton *(Orchestration)*; Frank Larue *(Miss Taylor's Makeup)*; John Jiras *(Mr. Beatty's Makeup)*; Alexandre of Paris *(Miss Taylor's Hairstyles)*; Claude Ettori *(Hair Stylist)*; Ed-

gar Lansbury *(Producer for New York stage version)*; The Chrysler Corporation *(Boats furnished)*. Color by Deluxe.

Opened March 4, 1970, at the Penthouse and Showcase Theatres, New York, N.Y. Running time, 113 minutes.

The Only Game in Town was a negative experience for Beatty in most respects. He did come out of it well financially, nicking the producers for $750,000. His co-star was the ailing, unpredictable Elizabeth Taylor (their one and only appearance together) and *she* got $1,250,000. The picture wound up with a negative cost of

A tender moment between
Elizabeth Taylor and Beatty

Taylor and Beatty contemplate the joys of felicitous bedmanship.

Taylor kibitzes while Beatty clowns.

$10,000,000 and pulled in only about a million and a half. Production was delayed time and again by Taylor's assorted illnesses (an operation for a female condition was followed by a recurrence of her old disc problems from a 1957 spinal operation). Taylor and Frank Sinatra were announced in April 1968 as the co-stars of this 20th Century-Fox picturization of Frank Gilroy's short-lived Broadway play (sixteen performances) for which 20th had paid Gilroy $500,000. Though Tammy Grimes and Barry Nelson had been winning in the leads, no one in Hollywood understood why this slight human-interest piece about a forlorn showgirl and a compulsive gambler in Las Vegas should be worth such an amount.

Miss Taylor's uterine operation necessitated a delay in shooting, and in September 1968 Frank Sinatra withdrew from the cast pleading a prior engagement that could not await Taylor's recovery. Taylor's weight ballooned, thus adding to her other problems. Production finally began in October 1968 with eighty-six days of shooting in Paris, then ten days of shooting in Las Vegas, capped by a final week at 20th Century-Fox Studios in Hollywood, where interior shots were completed. By this time it was February 1969. The George Stevens–directed film was not released for a year after that, opening around the country in the early months of 1970. It was a box-office disaster and was yanked out of theatres in a week or so, before it had a chance to pick up whatever audience would have been interested. Over the long run, *The Only Game in Town* lost about $7,000,000.

Miss Taylor had insisted on Paris shooting for most of the film, so as to be near her husband Richard Burton, who was shooting *Staircase* with Rex Harrison in that city. This involved incalculable additional expense, as 20th's art and prop departments had to import furniture and appurtenances from Las Vegas—but Queen Liz's whims were law and Paris it was.

Beatty found himself catering to someone other than himself for a change, and had to humor Taylor's moods, assuring her how beautiful she was and waiting patiently for her indispositions to run their course. At $750,000, he wasn't in an unduly complaining or testy mood throughout the shooting, and considering their respective temperaments, Beatty and Taylor got along quite well. George Stevens directed meticulously, if

slowly, fussing over details, and much was made publicly of his career reunion with Taylor, the two having worked to much acclaim in *A Place in the Sun* and *Giant* back in the 1950s. But unfortunately neither Stevens—famed for his human-interest-laden, sentimental-yet-realistic films such as *Alice Adams* and *Woman of the Year,* landmarks of the 30s and 40s respectively—nor his feminine star were at their best. Time and inactivity had eroded Stevens's directorial touch and he had become ponderous and heavy-handed. Taylor, plagued by illnesses and weight problems, gave a listless, offhand performance, and she and Beatty were both rather flagrantly miscast. She was not any right-minded person's conception of a forlorn, wistful showgirl waiting around for a married man to divorce his wife, and Beatty lacked the gritty incisiveness required for the compulsive gambler. Ginger Rogers and Cary Grant would have waltzed through it thirty years before, especially had they been guided by a Stevens then in his professional prime, but by now the net result had an old-fashioned look. Sex was kept to a decorous minimum, there was no nudity, and in 1969–70 exhibitors were interested only in sex fare that could be exploited salaciously. The whole concept was too tame and wistful and low-keyed. The story of two sad people in Las Vegas who turn to each other out of loneliness, with the Beatty character winning and losing large sums at gambling and finding himself unable to eliminate his compulsion even at the expense of Taylor's love, was too intimate, confined, and introspective for audiences of 1970, whom TV violence and jangling, fast-paced montage techniques had corrupted to the point where they wanted to be fed sensations rather than illuminative human truths.

But the audience alone was not to blame for this fiasco. Despite some charitable, "tradey" reviews by the usual journalistic sycophants, some perceptive, independent-minded critics told it like it was, and the "was" of it was simply that *The Only Game in Town* was a dull, carelessly-tooled movie, too long at 113 minutes for the slight story it had to tell. The film did contain one of the more human and likeable characterizations of Beatty's more recent years; he may have lacked the bite the character required, but he did reveal a boyishly winning side his girlfriends had long insisted was there, but which he too often concealed from his public, at least in his films.

Beatty in the throes of the game

Gambling hath charms, as Beatty discovers to his cost.

Putting it on what he hopes is a lucky square

REVIEWS:

Bruce Bahrenburg in *The Newark Sunday News:* "Miss Taylor and Beatty make an excellent couple. She is shrill and brittle and he is wise and open. They play well together. The film is entertaining without being of any great consequence to the war in Vietnam or inflation at home. It is a pure Hollywood fabrication of a kind that worked well for [director George] Stevens in the 1940s, and though it is too long, it is entertaining. Why was it such a failure [in other cities], ripped out of circulation before it could find an audience, if there is still one for this type of romantic comedy? One possible answer is that it isn't dirty enough to be exploited in a salacious ad campaign. For the truth is that too many Hollywood money men rate the market value of a film on how much it can get away with short of a police raid. By this standard, with its absence of nudity and obscenity, Stevens's film is very tame. But it is more enjoyable in its innocent way than most films now at the neighborhood theatres."

Elaine Rothschild in *Films in Review:* "*The Only Game in Town* isn't about very much — merely how a Las Vegas chorus girl and a piano-player in a Vegas night-spot who is addicted to gambling finally say to each other: 'I love you.' Indeed, it is about so little one wonders why George Stevens chose it as the vehicle for his return to directing after his debacle with *The Greatest Story Ever Told.* I assume Elizabeth Taylor agreed to play the chorine out of loyalty to Stevens, who directed her in *A Place in the Sun* and *Giant.* Given the participation of Stevens and Taylor, Warren Beatty's reason for playing the piano player is obvious (he was a second choice — Sinatra had to withdraw when production was postponed). Miss Taylor is still a beautiful woman, and the clothes designed for this film by Mia Fonssagrives and Vicki Tiel do her justice. Director Stevens is still a meticulous craftsman, and no programmer has ever been put on the screen more lucidly (the screenplay was by Frank D. Gilroy from his play). Believe it or not, Stevens almost got a performance out of Beatty. Watching Elizabeth Taylor perform under the aegis of a director as good as Stevens is a pleasant, and not altogether a profitless, way to spend two hours."

Elizabeth Taylor listens meditatively to pianist Beatty's rendition.

154

McCabe & Mrs. Miller

CAST:
Warren Beatty *(John McCabe)*; Julie Christie *(Constance Miller)*; Rene Auberjonois *(Sheehan)*; John Schuck *(Smalley)*; Bert Remsen *(Burt Coyle)*; Keith Carradine *(Cowboy)*; William Devane *(The Lawyer)*; Corey Fischer *(Mr. Elliott)*; Shelley Duvall *(Ida Coyle)*; Michael Murphy *(Sears)*; Anthony Holland *(Hollander)*; Tom Hill *(Archer)*; Don Francks *(Buffalo)*; Rodney Gage *(Summer Washington)*; Lili Francks *(Mrs. Washington)*; Hugh Millais, Manfred Schulz, Jace Vander Veen *(Killers)*; Jackie Crossland, Elizabeth

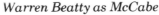

Warren Beatty as McCabe

Beatty and Christie discuss business.

Murphy, Carey Lee McKenzie (*Bearpaw Whores*); Linda Sorense, Elizabeth Knight, Janet Wright (*Seattle Whores*); Maysie Hoy (*Maisie*); Linda Kupecek (*Ruth*); Jeremy Newsom (*Jeremy Berg*); Wayne Robson (*Bartender*); Jack Riley (*Riley Quinn*); Robert Fortier (*Town Drunk*); Wayne Grace (*Bartender*); Wesley Taylor (*Shorty Dunn*); Anne Cameron (*Mrs. Dunn*); Graeme Campbell (*Bill Cubbs*); J.S. Johnson (*J.J.*); Joe Clarke (*Joe Shortreed*); Harry Frazier (*Andy Anderson*); Edwin Collier (*Gilchrist*); Terence Kelly (*Quirley*); Brantley F. Kearns (*Fiddler*).

CREDITS:
A Robert Altman–David Foster Production; David Foster and Mitchell Brower (*Producers*); Robert Altman (*Director*); Louis Lombardo (*2nd Unit Director*); Robert Altman and Brian McKay (*Screenplay*); Based on the novel *McCabe* by Edmund Naughton; Vilmos Zsigmond (*Photographer*); Rod Parkhurst (*Second Unit Photography*); Leonard Cohen (*Songs*); Leon Ericksen (*Production Designer and Costume Supervisor*); Philip Thomas and Al Locatelli (*Art Directors*); Marcel Vercoutere (*Special Effects*); Anthony Goldschmidt (*Titles*); Barry Jones, John V. Gusselle and William A. Thompson (*Sound*); Robert Jiras, Ed Butterworth and Phyllis Newman (*Hairstyles*); Barry Richardson (*Associate Producer*); Robert Eggenweiler (*Associate Producer*); James Marcellos (*Production Manager*); Tommy Thompson and Irby Smith (*Assistant Directors*); Panavision. Color by Technicolor.

Opened at selected theaters in New York, June 24, 1971. Running time, 120 minutes.

Beatty did not make another film for two years after *The Only Game in Town*. Since that film had done so poorly at the box office, he doubtless decided that attempts at human sentiment with sex played down were not what the public wanted to see. His new film, *McCabe & Mrs. Miller*, was, however, an unfortunate example of going from one extreme to another. The film was directed by Robert Altman, who had made something of a name for himself with such films as *M*A*S*H* and *Brewster McCloud*, in which he had demonstrated a vivid mastery of striking and illuminating detail, but McCabe had a trashy, pointless plot and was directed in so (admittedly) experi-

mental and pseudo-impressionist a manner that its point was blunted and its effect dissipated.

McCabe was shot on location in West Vancouver, British Columbia, over a period of several months. Photographer Vilmos Zsigmond was allowed to cut loose with a lot of tricky, pseudo-arty photography that called too much attention to itself, and while all kinds of weather is caught in some striking shots, the story purposes are neither furthered nor clarified. Altman, who had long been in rebellion against the limitations on spontaneous inspiration imposed by union-dominated economics, decided to cut loose in free-form style in telling his story, but the net result was obscurantist and tendentious rather than moving, illuminating or cathartic. The critics of the day, searching frantically for something to like about the film, and aware that it had cost a mint to put out, fell over themselves praising its alleged realism, its debunking of the Western myth, its cynicism, its atmospheric effects, etc., but the truest statement, and the most honest was probably made by *Films in Review*'s Henry Hart, who said in part: "The cinematic incompetence of director-scripter Robert Altman is all too visible in this immature farrago of ignorantly conceived characters and 'symbolic' situations. It's true Altman only collaborated on the script (with Brian McKay from a novel, *McCabe* by Edmund Naughton) but even if McKay is responsible for this film's lack of understanding of frontier life, and of the rudiments of dramaturgy and characterization, Altman must be blamed for going ahead with a senseless script. And he's solely to blame for incompetent and pretentious direction." Hart went on to point out the film's "social irresponsibility," its tendency to "propagandize for the drug cop-out that currently wastes the youth of so many of the today generation." Beatty "fell on his face" as an actor, Hart added, and Julie Christie "is still worthy of better things than attempting, under Altman's witless supervision, to play a whore-madam the like of which was never seen in West or East."

Much was made of the fact that in attempting to meet the deadline for the first scheduled East and West Coast screenings, Warners rushed two prints of the film from a processing laboratory in Canada—too hastily, it turned out, for the color and sound were badly garbled and flawed. The critics who saw the defective version turned in

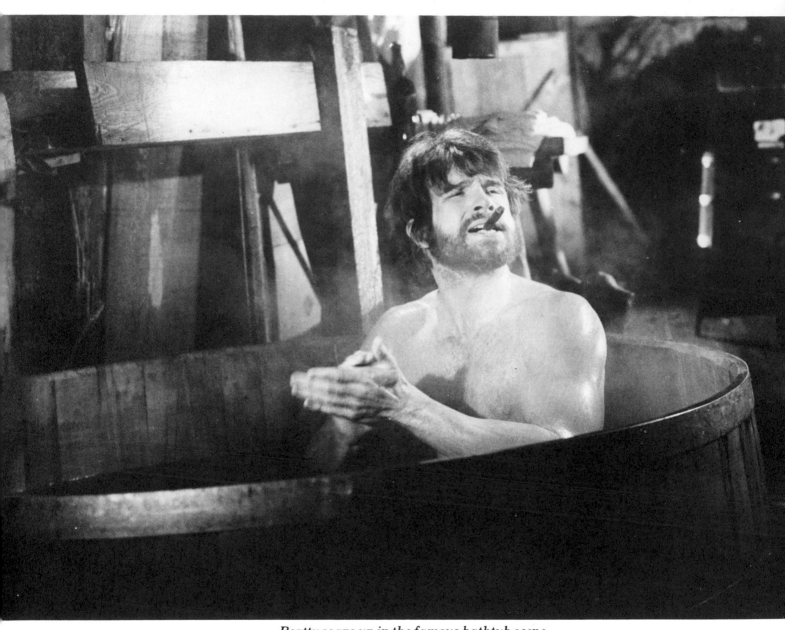

Beatty soaps up in the famous bathtub scene.

Beatty during the building of the town

A thoughtful interlude for Beatty and Christie

initially unfavorable reviews, then were made to see still another version, technically perfect, which caused them to alter their reactions from unfavorable to favorable. Since *McCabe & Mrs. Miller* is a very poor film even when technically up to snuff, it is hard to believe that any critic in his right mind would have changed his opinion. The whole incident, reported tongue-in-cheek style in the press that year, smacked of manipulative studio tactics and monkey-business with critical approaches—all that money was riding on the film, you know. This was a rare instance of monkey-business between studio and critics *coming to the surface;* there should be more.

Meanwhile director Altman was giving out such statements to the press as: "I just wanted to take a very standard Western story with a classic story line and do it real or what I felt was real, and destroy all the myths of heroism." Moscow couldn't have asked for more, and no doubt sneaked-in prints of *McCabe & Mrs. Miller* have been shown to Russian opinion-makers within the borders of the Soviet Union as an example of how corrupt and degraded American pioneers really were!

The story line? Beatty plays McCabe, a small-time gambler who pretends to a past as a gunman. He moves into Presbyterian Church (a pretentious name for a boom town) and with poker winnings buys property and sets up a whorehouse. Then an opium-addicted madam (Julie Christie) shows up and offers to help Beatty ex-

160

pand the bordello with classier girls from Seattle and a more professional conduct of affairs, with the profits split between them. A big corporation wants to move in, and when Beatty rejects their original offer, they decide to take over by force. The church burns down, Christie takes refuge in drugs, and Beatty is shot and dies in a snowdrift after a running battle with the hired gunmen sent in to rub him out. So much for the plot.

Sporting moustache, beard and bowler hat, Beatty tried to offer his idea of a sporty Western character of 1902 vintage. In fairness to him, he seems to have invested McCabe with considerable thought, and there are more well-conceived details and nuances in his performance than usual. One can't fault an actor for trying to stretch his creative potential. But considering the limitations of the script and direction, even John Wayne couldn't have made McCabe resemble a human being.

But the famous Beatty star charisma was on full force; at thirty-four he looked extremely handsome in some of the shots, and he does get points for attempted inventiveness, some of which registered.

REVIEWS:
Pauline Kael in *The New Yorker:*
"McCabe & Mrs. Miller is a beautiful pipedream of a movie — a fleeting, almost diaphanous vision of what frontier life might have been . . . it's not much like other Westerns; it's not really much like other movies . . . it seems so strange because, despite a great deal of noise about the art of film, we are unaccustomed to an intuitive, quixotic, essentially impractical approach to moviemaking, and to an exploratory approach to a subject, particularly when the subject is the American past. . . . The picture is testimony to the power of stars. Warren Beatty and Julie Christie have never been better, and they are the two most interesting people . . . they seem to take over the screen by

Beatty escorting the new whores

natural right—because we want to look at them longer and more closely . . . it's hard to know what makes Beatty such a magnetic presence; he was that even early in his screen career. Now that he has developed pace and control, he has become just about as attractive a screen star as any of the romantic heroes of the past. He has an unusually comic romantic presence; there's a gleefulness in Beatty, a light that comes on when he is on screen that says, 'Watch this—it's fun!' . . . a fresh, ingenious performance."

Arthur Knight in *The Saturday Review:*
"Funny, sad, touching, and curiously moral as well. Warren Beatty's half-truculent, half-aggrieved under-the-breath mutterings are both amusing and touching when contrasted to, rather than merged with, the strangled, semiarticulate patterns of his normal speech as McCabe."

Vincent Canby in *The New York Times:*
"The intentions of *McCabe & Mrs. Miller* are not

only serious, they are also meddlesome, imposed on the film by tired symbolism, by a folk-song commentary on the sound track that recalls not the old Pacific Northwest but San Francisco's "hungry i" and by the sort of metaphysically purposeful photography that, in a tight closeup, attempts to discover the soul secrets in the iris of an eye and finds, instead, only a very large iris. Such intentions keep spoiling the fun of what might have been an uproarious frontier fable. . . . Beatty's gambler-turned-businessman is a truly comic, clay-footed entrepreneur, and Miss Christie's tough-talking whore is about as appealing as that sentimental character can be until she's required to drift off into opium oblivion, a woman-turned-into-society's-victim . . . Altman fills his screen with sometimes exceptionally vivid detail, such as the casually viewed fight between a knife-wielding prostitute and her customer."

Charles Champlin in *The Los Angeles Times:*
"The Warren Beatty portrayal is colorful—cigar-

Beatty busy card-sharping.

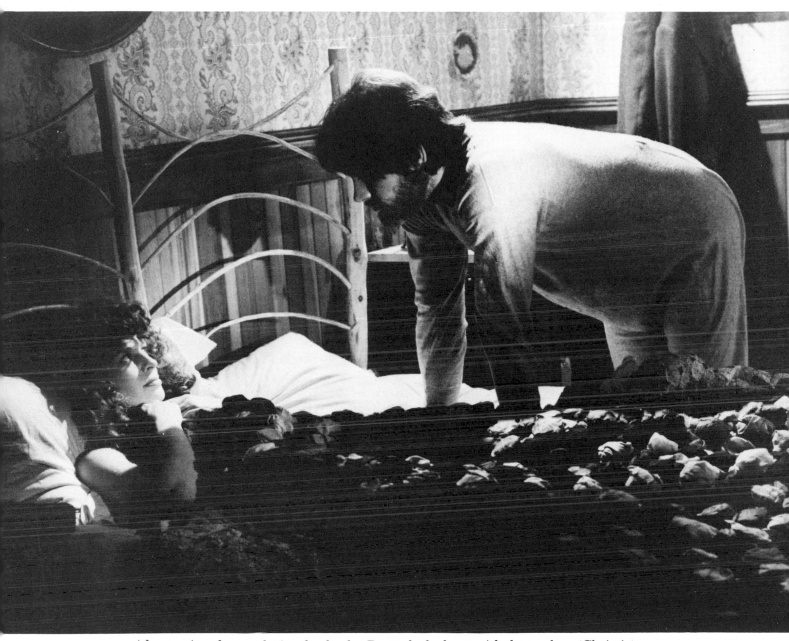

After paying the regulation five bucks, Beatty beds down with the madam (Christie)

Christie gives Beatty her side of things.

chomping, egg-gulping, teeth-baring, squinting, lurching—but it has a lot less consistency than Miss Christie's. He's an anti-hero, of course, drawn into a showdown because there's no escape. But it's not ever clear whether he's clever enough to be a con man or dumb enough to be a nice guy . . . there is less [about the film] than meets the eye, although what meets the eye is generally entertaining, often vivid—and looks to have been grueling hard work to get on film. It becomes a star vehicle, and the charm of its principals obscures the sardonic and corrective view of the past which, if I am right, the movie had been intended to take."

Films in Review:
"The cinematic incompetence of director-scripter Robert Altman is all too visible in this immature farrago of ignorantly conceived characters amid "symbolic" situations . . . a lack of understanding of frontier life, and of the rudiments of dramaturgy and characterization. Altman must be blamed for going ahead with a senseless script. And he's solely to blame for incompetent and pretentious direction . . . it is fitting that Warren Beatty should fall on his face attempting to play the pimpish gambler who, in this 121-minute depressant, runs a whorehouse in a primitive settlement tendentiously called Presbyterian Church. But the once promising Julie Christie is still worthy of better things than attempting, under Altman's witless supervision, to play a whoremadam the like of which was never seen in West or East."

164

$ (Dollars)

CAST:

Warren Beatty *(Joe Collins)*; Goldie Hawn *(Dawn Divine)*; Gert Frobe *(Mr. Kessel)*; Robert Webber *(Attorney)*; Scott Brady *(Sarge)*; Arthur Brauss *(Candy Man)*; Robert Stiles *(Major)*; Wolfgang Kieling *(Granich)*; Robert Herron *(Bodyguard)*; Christiane Maybach *(Helga)*; Hans Hutter *(Karl)*; Monica Stender *(Betta)*; Françoise Blanc *(Stripper)*; Walt Trott *(Stars & Stripes Reporter)*; Darrell Armstrong *(A.P. Reporter)*; Horst Hesslein *(Bruno)*; Wolfgang Kuhlman *(Furcoat)*; Klaus Tschichan *(Knifeman)*; Tove Platon and Kirstein Lahman *(Customs Officials)*.

CREDITS:

An M.J. (Mike) Frankovich Production. M.J. Frankovich *(Producer)*; Richard Brooks *(Director and Writer)*; Petrus Schloemp *(Photographer)*; Quincy Jones *(Music)*; Songs "Money Is" and "Do It to It" sung by Little Richard; "When You're Smiling," composed by Mark Fisher, Joe Goodwin and Larry Shay, sung by Roberta Flack; George Grenville *(Editor)*; Guy Sheppard and Olaf Ivens *(Art Directors)*; Arthur Piantadosi, Richard Tyler and Jack Haynes *(Sound)*; Johannes Kohner *(Wardrobe)*; Ernest Schmekel and Bob Jiras *(Makeup)*; Berry Richardson *(Hair Styles)*; Tom Shaw *(Assistant Director)*. Color by Technicolor.

Opened at the Loew's State and Tower East Theatres, New York, December 15, 1971. Running time, 119 minutes.

Advertisement for $

Warren Beatty watches Goldie Hawn count all that lovely moola.

Satisfying his restless wanderlust, Beatty took off for Scandinavia, Bavaria and Hamburg for location filming of *$ (Dollars)*, which Richard Brooks wrote and directed. Brooks, of *Brothers Karamazov* and *In Cold Blood* fame, not to mention earlier blockbusters like the 1958 *Cat on a Hot Tin Roof,* was regarded by more than one critic as too serious and artistically conscientious a director for such a frivolous, fluffy "caper" confection as *$*, which he had also written. The *$* title was a "cutesy" gimmick that Columbia tried to milk to the ultimate, with publicity copy to the effect that *$* meant not dollar or dollar sign but dollars plural, and the New York *Daily News* critic went along with the gag by giving the film four *$* instead of the customary stars.

Again Beatty came in for severe criticism for wasting his energies in a caper film reminiscent of more than a few that had gone before, and again the suspicion was voiced that he took trivial action-and-spoof fare in order not to tax his acting energies or potentials, however limited or great *those* might be.

Beatty made the most of his "vacation" film among interesting European sites, and kept his private life going full blast as usual. Goldie Hawn played opposite him; she had won an Oscar for *Cactus Flower* in 1969, then played a tart in *There's a Girl in My Soup.* Now again she was playing a tart with a dollar sign for a heart, who gets involved with "caper-cat" Beatty in a bank heist that is ingeniously planned, or anyway as ingenious and original as writer Brooks could make it. There were critical complaints that Hawn was getting into a "tart-rut" casting-wise, and while Beatty's performance was called "affable" and "filled with star magnetism," it was obvious he would be no threat to any 1971 Oscar contenders. Indeed, he seemed to coast through the role, skimming along on the surface, albeit

$ $ $ all over the place for a gleeful Beatty and Hawn

Warren begins wondering if Goldie is taking her work too seriously.

with lots of physical gymnastics, but making little or no effort to flex his thespian muscles. He smiles a lot, makes love with Beatty-style éclat when the busy plot doings permit, and at the end plays mouse to the cat — or rather rat to the cat — across a frozen lake until the villain's car sinks through the ice — a suspenseful touch, but much too long and drawn out, indeed excruciating in length.

The fun in caper films of this type lies in the action, and the plot can be recapitulated briefly. American security expert Beatty steals the contents of three safe deposit boxes from a Hamburg, Germany, bank; they are owned by crooks of varying styles and persuasions who are in no position

to complain to the authorities. Beatty's chance comes while installing a new alarm system; a Hamburg whore and former Vegas showgirl (Hawn) aids and abets him because she likes his looks and likes the color green. After a bomb scare, Beatty persuades bank officials to lock him in the vault, where he stashes away the contents of three boxes into one Hawn has rented. Then out she walks with the swag. The fleeced crooks are soon in pursuit, and then comes that interminable frozen-lake episode.

"Why doesn't Warren Beatty face up to his responsibilities as an important star and come out with more solid stuff than this?" one commentator wrote in 1971, and her stridently articulated

Warren with bag of money during the famous ice chase sequence

question was indeed a good one. The events of the next year, 1972, would demonstrate that the politics-conscious — indeed politics-obsessed — Beatty, who was to be active in the McGovern presidential campaign, took his politics much more seriously than his filmic art — and many Beatty-watchers publicly asked: Why? Beatty stayed off the screen for two and a half years after this trivial film, and another writer wanted to know — this was by now 1973 — why Beatty couldn't show his serious side as actor and movie entrepreneur as readily as he did on the political front.

The sex in $ is on the vulgar side; Hawn's first shot shows her backside in transparent underwear as a tired, old-looking Scott Brady, a crooked army sergeant who specializes in heroin deals and PX thieving, slips money into said transparent underwear. Arthur Brauss is arresting as Candy Man, whose Thing is the transportation of pure LSD in champagne bottles, and the other villain, Robert Webber, is properly ominous in manner and tone as an American lawyer who has vaulted tax-and-syndicate ill-gotten gains. Gert Frobe is in good form as Kessel, a bank official who plays into Superthief Beatty's hands.

The critical reaction to $ was distinctly on the divided side, veering toward the negative. "Pretentious" was an adjective thrown at the film by more than one critic, followed closely by "overwritten," with one critic complaining that for the first twenty minutes he didn't know what the hell was going on — and by the twenty-first minute couldn't have cared less.

Beatty has himself a narcissistic field day in this, grinning slyly and purveying charm for all comers, wearing his suits with a carelessly calculated flair. He told one reporter that $ was a picture designed to entertain, that it represented a departure for Brooks who needed on occasion to be cinematically frivolous as well as the frequently serious filmmaker he had shown himself

Gert Frobe and Warren Beatty in a tense phone moment.

Beatty and Goldie Hawn cogitate over the misdeeds.

to be in the past, and to everybody's satisfaction. Asked if he didn't want to do more serious things, Beatty pointed to the dearth of ideas and themes calculated to enlighten and entertain at the same time, said *$* was the best thing he had found available at the time. When one reporter asked why he didn't search more diligently for worthwhile material, he challenged the reporter to go out and find "worthwhile fare" and told him it would be a tougher hunt than he thought. Beatty, however, made his Columbia flacks happy by saying he thought *$* had turned out pretty well, all things considered, had given him a chance to tour some interesting European sites, and "could have been worse," adding: "I have no apologies to tender anyone, anywhere, any time."

REVIEWS:

Gary Arnold in *The Washington Post:*

"Decidedly sour—disorganized—dismally facetious. Warren Beatty . . . remains cute, but is wasting his and our time (when he read the screenplay, didn't it occur to him that it was *Kaleidoscope* all over again, only worse?). Goldie Hawn [suggests] a neurotic sheepdog and [is] rapidly twitching her way into oblivion. Having come a cropper with 'serious' material the last time out—the sincere, misbegotten, unmourned *The Happy Ending*—writer-director Richard Brooks reverses his field and goes totally frivolous and mercenary . . . judging by *$*, his frivolous bent is as treacherous and disagreeable as his serious one . . . This hectic attempt at generating

Beatty begins monkeying at the Hamburg bank vault.

fun-fun-fun is mercenary, all right, but it's inept and distasteful . . . One of the most annoying aspects of the movie is Brooks's failure to establish either the characters or the gimmick until one's patience has worn thin with all his tiresomely busy, gratuitous direction, which is designed to mystify us and succeeds in exactly the wrong way, by making it impossible for us to enjoy or savor Beatty's criminal smartness. By the time his plan is defined, the movie has become fairly alienating and exhausting . . . Beatty can probably take this inferior vehicle in stride, but one must feel very apprehensive about Goldie Hawn's future in the movies."

Charles Champlin in *The Los Angeles Times:*
"Richard Brooks's *$* is a crackling good crime-

chase-suspense story. Its considerable pleasure is that it sets us solidly in a colorful, unfamiliar but unquestionably real place—Hamburg, Germany—and plays its ingenious charades absolutely as if they were part of the teeming life of that city . . . Brooks as a filmmaker is a meticulous craftsman, strongly independent and issue-oriented. In *$* as in his slambang Western, *The Professionals,* he has made the issues secondary to some uninhibited storytelling [and] has provided a well-nigh classic formulation for a thriller . . . The performances are predictably smooth. Warren Beatty makes the most of his star charm."

Roger Greenspun in *The New York Times:*
"'They're spoofing! They're spoofing! He, he!'" chortled a woman in the row behind me at the

preview screening. But she was chortling in the dark, because they weren't spoofing, at least not the way she meant. Halfway through the climax to Richard Brooks's $ with Warren Beatty trapped on thin ice (literally) I think all of us would have taken a joke at any level to escape the strenuous and interminable chase sequence that spells coronaries for the cast, ennui for the audience and the elephantine enlargement of what had been an amiable little caper movie . . . Amia-

ble little caper movies are not so common these days that I should care to write off any one of them. Furthermore $ boasts an attractive cast, some clever dialogue (also by Brooks) and lots of suspense — at least until the chase begins and seems never to end, and you wish that everyone would go home and get some rest. $ is actually a decent short film that has been made long by the most predictable and least ingenious of means . . . Everybody does well."

Beatty and the bank personnel consider the ominous situation.

Warren Beatty

The Parallax View

CAST:
Warren Beatty *(Joseph Frady)*; Hume Cronyn *(Edgar Rintels)*; William Daniels *(Austin Tucker)*; Paula Prentiss *(Lee Carter)*; Kelly Thordsen *(Sheriff)*; Earl Hindman *(Deputy)*; Kenneth Mars *(Former FBI agent)*; Walter McGinn *(Parallax Representative)*; Jim Davis *(Senator Hammond)*; Bill Joyce *(Senator Carroll)*; Bill McKinney *(Assassin)*; William Jordan *(Tucker's Aide)*; Stacy Keach and Ford Rainey *(Commission Spokesmen)*.

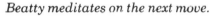

Beatty meditates on the next move.

Newscaster Paula Prentiss has her doubts about the assassination.

Giving the heavy the business

CREDITS:

A Gus Production in Association with Harbor Productions. Alan J. Pakula *(Producer and Director);* David Giler, Lorenzo Semple, Jr. *(Screenplay);* Based on the novel by Loren Singer; Gordon Willis *(Photographer);* John W. Wheeler *(Editor);* Michael Small *(Music);* George Jenkins *(Production Designer);* Reg Allen *(Set Decorations);* David Dockendorf, Bud Grenzbach, Tom Overton *(Sound);* Howard W. Koch, Jr. *(Assistant Director);* Color by Technicolor.

Opened at the Cinema I Theatre, New York, June 19, 1974. Running time, 102 minutes.

After two years of cinematic inactivity during which Beatty had his fling with politics, he returned to the screen in *The Parallax View.* The film's release was delayed for months after it was "in the can"; when it debuted in June 1974, Beatty had not had a picture in the nation's movie houses for a full two and a half years. The picture's political angle was doubtless the deciding factor in his choice, since that was the ambience in which he had chosen to immerse himself for such a considerable time.

After a presidential candidate is assassinated, a committee investigating the deed announces that it was the act of one deranged individual and not a conspiracy. But when a number of witnesses die under rather mysterious circumstances, a newscaster (Paula Prentiss) begins to wonder what's going on. She tells reporter Beatty about her impressions, after which she, too, joins the list of sudden victims. Beatty starts an in-depth inquiry of his own, and after undergoing a vari-

Beatty is aware of someone behind him.

Walter McGinn catches Beatty enjoying a quiet drink.

ety of action-and-suspense-oriented vicissitudes, arrives at the solution: a powerful combine named Parallax has carefully chosen assassins via responses to specially rigged, psychologically illuminative questionnaires, then dispatches its murderous puppets to eliminate figures "on their list."

Assigned to direct was Alan J. Pakula, who also produced. *Parallax* was Pakula's fourth directorial stint, following *The Sterile Cuckoo* with Liza Minnelli, *Klute* with Jane Fonda, and the romantic *Love and Pain and the Whole Damn Thing*. Based on a novel of Loren Singer, *Parallax* bore more than a passing resemblance to *The Manchurian Candidate*, which also dealt with puppet assassins, but did not have the quality or polish of that earlier film. *The Parallax View* also boasted, as did the novel, one of those tricky titles so dear to the hearts of latter-day novelists and filmmakers. Parallax, according to the dictionary, is "the apparent change in the position of an object resulting from the change in the direction or position from which it is viewed."

Beatty contributed a well-thought-out, multidimensional performance as the reporter who uncovers the truth at considerable personal cost; he registers the required tension and alertness of response to the various dangers to which he is subjected en route to the denouement, which despite the assorted artifices of director-producer Pakula and screenwriters David Giler and Lorenzo Semple, Jr., is reasonably predictable, as these excursions into politically oriented and flavored melodrama often are.

Pakula enjoys extensive analyses of his pictures, as given to journalists interested enough to probe him for the whys and wherefores. He has credited his photographer, Gordon Willis, with understanding his intentions from the start and giving them visual articulation. Pakula has said that he decided from the beginning that he and Willis would shoot only in locales that provided "a sense of the bizarre contrasts we take for granted in our society." Determined that his assassinations (there is one at the beginning, one later, both of Senators) would have a counterpointing background of what he termed "authentic Americana," he chose Seattle for its famed Space Needle, a futuristic symbol left over from Seattle's 1962 World's Fair. What Pakula also found arresting was an Indian totem pole, which he and

Willis found they could get into the same range as the Space Needle, thus dramatically contrasting the American past and present. "I also wanted to suggest the polyglot character of American life," he added, and found the perfect thing in Seattle's Chinese Girls' Drill Team, which Willis photographed with interestingly original effects.

Pakula showed that he could guide contrapuntal, variegated action scenes, welding them together with clever editing to keep the pace moving crisply. There are a number of good scenes, especially one featuring Walter McGinn and Beatty, during which Beatty plays a game of wits, chess-style, with prober McGinn while the latter is subjecting him to a five-minute psychological test to find out if Beatty has the required "psychopathically puppetish" qualities to function as an easily-controlled and directed assassin. The fencing between the two (this was the talented Walter McGinn's most effective film appearance after many fine stage performances) was electric, well-paced and skillfully guided by Pakula and Willis to squeeze maximum tension out of just a few minutes. Paula Prentiss is interesting but slightly miscast as the news hen who pays with her life for her curiosity, and Hume Cronyn makes the most of his few scenes as a newspaper editor.

The Parallax View got a hospitable reception from critics and public; it was not one of Beatty's more solid hits, but he chose it reportedly because he felt it blended solid action potential with an always-timely political theme—assassinations and their whys and wherefores. Beatty, Pakula and others concerned with the film went out of their way to stress that it was not based on the Kennedy murders, though the parallels were obvious. Pakula has defined his directorial technique as "leaving nothing to chance. Every frame in my film must contribute to communication of my original idea; they are the result of careful and comprehensive planning." He adds: "I have always felt one develops one's style for a film in the work itself. The first time I read a script, or if we start with a book or an idea, I begin to shape a conception. I did not want *The Parallax View* to be a documentary. I was not doing an exposé of what actually happened in the Kennedy assassination. I deliberately set out to stage a fictitious assassination for just that reason: so that it would be taken as sort of an American myth based on

In a heavy confab with Kenneth Mars

Hiding from the pursuer

Talking it over with another character

Park bench consultation with Walter McGinn

some things that have happened, some fantasies we may have had of what might have happened, and a lot of fears many of us have had.

The Parallax View, as Pakula intended, does give an indication, and a strong one, of the contrasts in American life, and has, due to Willis's imaginative camerawork and Pakula's wide-ranging concept, a kind of bizarre showiness.

Pakula worked with Beatty and the other actors in what he has styled as "a loose way. I work in different ways with different actors. I try to do it in a way that is right for the star and his co-workers. I discuss it with the leading actors beforehand to reach an accommodation, to make certain that we are all striving for the same concept." Beatty and Pakula had what they termed "healthy disagreements" during the filming, but worked together quite well in the main, with the result that Pakula got from Beatty one of his better performances of recent years.

REVIEWS:
Michael Buckley in *Films in Review:*
"In his first screen appearance since *McCabe & Mrs. Miller,* Warren Beatty makes an attractive screen hero, though he still speaks monosyllabically. His role, poorly defined, is still larger than any other two herein combined (perhaps explaining why Beatty's is the only name in opening credits). . . . based on Loren Singer's novel of the same title, *The Parallax View . . .* often resembles *The Manchurian Candidate* gone domestic. In no way superior to *The Manchurian Candidate,* the film is vastly more entertaining than the recent theory-as-fact *Executive Action."*

A tender moment with Paula Prentiss

Richard Schickel in *Time:*
"Played with a certain cheeky energy by Warren Beatty . . . as he proved in *Klute*, Pakula has a restless eye for the banalities of daily life that gives the picture a richer texture than is usual in this genre. Early on, the film offers some promise. There is a brisk barroom brawl and a short car chase that is more smartly handled than these maneuvers usually are. But there is no way to build an overparanoid thriller or to provide a satisfactory ending. If the hero can break the conspiracy unaided, it cannot be much of a conspiracy. If, on the other hand, the conspiracy is all-powerful then the audience is robbed of the basic pleasure of identifying with the protagonist's triumph over the odds. Pakula opts for the latter resolution in *Parallax*, and it is a downer. Though a touch of paranoid fantasizing can energize an entertainment, too much of it is just plain crazy — neither truthful nor useful. And certainly nothing for responsible men to try to make a buck with in the movies."

Paul D. Zimmerman in *Newsweek:*
"Adapted with great crispness and intelligence . . . for all its political references, the film is most impressive as a dazzling exercise in montage and melodrama. The psychologically adroit Pakula of *The Sterile Cuckoo* and *Klute* here blossoms into a first-rate stylist whose professionalism and technical acumen — backed by superbly chosen support troops — characterize American filmmaking at its best. Pakula has picked his locations with a perfectionist's care . . . Beatty, in a fine, low-keyed and bemused performance, is himself an outsider — a lone wolf — who with a change of con-

text can be taken for a killer. Pakula closes his movie as he opened it, with a wide-angled shot of a high, remote tribunal dismissing a new political assassination as the work of a single crazed killer. It is the burden of the scene and the film that America has refused to pursue its political killers for fear of finding that they are not peripheral pariahs but are intimately connected to us and our way of life. It is only after the film has released us from its spell that we wonder whether melodrama is the proper forum for raising such profound and unsettling questions."

Grieving over Paula Prentiss in the morgue

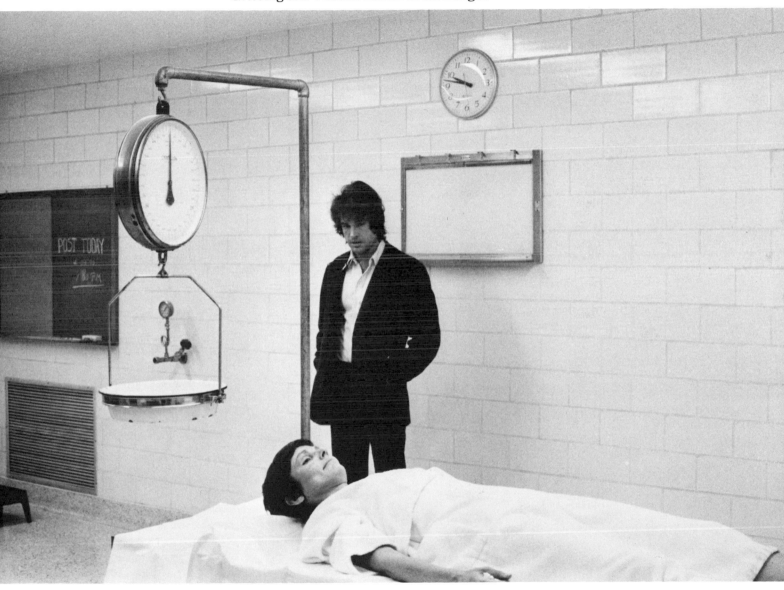

187

Beatty meditates while blinking into the sun.

Shampoo

Ad copy for Shampoo

CAST:
Warren Beatty *(George);* Julie Christie *(Jackie);* Goldie Hawn *(Jill);* Lee Grant *(Felicia);* Jack Warden *(Lester);* Tony Bill *(Johnny);* Carrie Fisher *(Lorna);* Jay Robinson *(Norman);* George Furth *(Bank Officer);* Brad Dexter *(Senator);* William Castle *(Producer).*

CREDITS:
Warren Beatty *(Producer);* Hal Ashby *(Director);* Warren Beatty and Robert Towne *(Screenplay);* Laszlo Kovacs *(Photographer);* Robert C. Jones *(Editor);* Paul Simon *(Music);* Richard Sylbert *(Production Designer);* Stuart Campbell *(Art Director);* George Gaines *(Set Decorator);* Tommy Overton *(Sound);* Art Levinson *(Assistant Director);* Color by Technicolor.

Opened at the Coronet Theatre, New York, February 11, 1975. Running time, 112 minutes.

A great deal has been written about Warren Beatty's *Shampoo;* the coverage reflects the over-inflated publicity and promotion which helped lift his earlier *Bonnie and Clyde* to critical and box-office fame. Both pictures were produced by Beatty, and he even helped to write *Shampoo,* a task he might better have left to a professional.
Shampoo is a real Freudian curio, and were Beatty the type to go in for heavy analysis, his psychiatrist would probably learn more about him from studying this film than from a year of pad-in-hand questioning.

With Julie Christie and Goldie Hawn

About to set out on a womanizing foray

The story of a Hollywood hairdresser who Don-Juans it indiscriminately around Beverly Hills boudoirs while giving the lady customers hair sets and what-not, *Shampoo* attempts to make the point that not all hairdressers are gay (which everyone knew anyway) and that not all Don Juan-compulsive heterosexuals are sublimating hatred of women and/or homosexual impulses. The latter point seemed of particular importance to Beatty, as per his public statements, doubtless because his own private-life Don Juaning with a host of women over the past eighteen years (while remaining a bachelor legally) just may (he feels) have been misconstrued.

Shampoo, like *Bonnie and Clyde,* has put more millions into Beatty's coffers. He thinks it unwise to discuss figures publicly, but as one wag put it, "With *Bonnie* he reportedly got *six* million; now, he must have *twelve* million, and since everything supposedly comes in threes, all Beatty now requires is a third picture that is aimed at the box-office jugular and cleverly promoted and hyped and he will have *eighteen* million!"

The critical reactions to *Shampoo* are interesting; while appearing to cover a broad spectrum of opinion, they arouse ever-growing suspicions that critics are easily-influenced sheep. *Time* put it forthrightly and independently, however, when it stated: "*Shampoo* is a problem. At its best moments, it is crafty, funny and high-spirited, but sometimes—even simultaneously—it is wormy and disingenuous. Just when a hard edge is crucial, the people who made it fall away from their best instincts and strongest insights into gross sentimentality."

There was some criticism of the forced and unwarranted setting of this stud-satyr-hairdresser's bedroom conquests at Election Time 1968, with

Julie Christie, Beatty and others in the famous dinner sequence

Beatty applies the famous blower to Julie Christie.

Nixon and Agnew dragged in for no purpose. So sleazy and pointless and silly a Hollywood stud-fest could take place in 1979, 1972, or 1932 for that matter. Human nature doesn't change. *Time* puzzled over this aspect, writing, "The reason, presumably, for setting the movie in 1968 is to groom George, the last shabby survivor of the age of grooviness, into a sardonic metaphor. There are many references to the Nixon election, and at times the movie appears to be attempting a delineation of the moral neutrality that could produce a Nixon and a Watergate."

But isn't the "Age of Grooviness" still flourishing in the late 1970s, and with a vengeance, as the more candid reports of doings in Hollywood and elsewhere amply attest? The simple truth is: *Shampoo* is a box-office-oriented depiction of the stud activities of a Hollywood hairdresser—the women he uses, the women who use him, the married women he plays around with, the girl he thinks he loves and who deserts him for a dirty (rich) old man, leaving him wallowing not so much in remorse as in self-pity.

There were a number of criticisms of the pseudo-sentimental ending, with Beatty mourning the departure of the one girl who presumably might have made a maturely caring, responsive man out of him, but since all that has gone before has dealt with a cynical stud whose brains are in his crotch and who substitutes a kind of stealth and self-protectiveness for any semblance of manly decency and clarity of character, mind and heart, no intelligent viewer can be in the least moved by Miss One and Only's desertion of him at the end.

But the sexy goings-on (Beatty gets fellated by Miss Christie under a table at dinner in a restaurant, where customers in formal attire try not to register shock) were sufficiently gamy to insure healthy returns, there were satirical touches, some of which hit home and some of which didn't, and Hal Ashby showed occasional inventiveness in his direction.

REVIEWS:
Marsha McCreadie in *Films in Review*:
"Significant satire or exploitative frippery? *Shampoo* has divided the critics, but one thing is certain—there is no neutral response to this intriguing concoction whipped up by Warren Beatty. . . . More questions are asked than answered about affluent California (read U.S.) life—from

wealthy business types to countercultural comforts—and about the now obvious national self-delusions which permitted a Nixon-Agnew victory . . . the broad, funny strokes of (George's) escapades show no winners . . . so much for being a Don Juan, even a swinger, in the late '60s. Yet that may be preferable to the more invidious forms of self-aggrandizement *Shampoo* dissects. And if that is where we were at then, *Shampoo* asks, where can we possibly be now?"

Jay Cocks in *Time*:
"*Shampoo* is a problem. At its best moments, it is crafty, funny and high-spirited, but sometimes—even simultaneously—it is wormy and disingenuous. Just when a hard edge is crucial, the people who made it fall away from their best instincts and strongest insight into gross sentimentality. As played, deftly, by Beatty, George is an affable con man who goes no deeper than his own hypocrisy. The reason, presumably, for setting the movie in 1968 is to groom George, the last, shabby survivor of the age of grooviness, into a sardonic metaphor . . . the ending is a betrayal of all that is best in the film, revealing that the film-makers have been interested in apologizing for George, not satirizing him. Still, much of *Shampoo* is good enough to make one regret its ultimate failure. The overpriced lassitude of Southern California living is well caught. Much of the dialogue has a keen edge. The acting . . . is well observed and sprightly. But *Shampoo* wants it both ways: wants a few laughs off George and wants, too, to bare his sensitive, desperate soul. It turns out that he is a figure looking for pity, and it hardly seems worth it."

Charles Champlin in *The Los Angeles Times*:
"*Shampoo* will be worth studying a century from now to know what a part of our times was like. Its language wipes out whatever reticences were left in the screen's playback of life as spoken. Its images manage fairly ingeniously to keep a few letters east of X and yet the combination of word and half-seen deed makes *Shampoo* seem more explicit than *Last Tango in Paris* and Warren Beatty out-reveals Marlon Brando by a few square inches of sacroiliac."

Frank Rich in *New Times*:
"[The film] is a terribly bright and laceratingly

witty recollection of where we were on that winnerless night; it's also a terribly jolting reminder of where we've been stuck ever since."

Aaron Schindler in *Family Circle:*
"*Shampoo* is a thoughtful, even poignant, portrait of a frightened man . . . Warren Beatty has never been more appealing. [The film] is that best of all possible filmic concoctions—one that keeps us entertained while we're seeing it, and then keeps us thinking about it for a long time afterwards."

Judith Crist in *New York Magazine:*
"The *La Dolce Vita* for the 1970s . . . Warren Beatty's *Shampoo,* a double-leveled work in his *Bonnie and Clyde* tradition, establishes the actor

as a serious-minded filmmaker with a cool eye on our society. This is his best comedy performance to date and his co-stars are dazzling. Under Hal Ashby's astute direction, *Shampoo* is a black-tinted comedy that touches memorably and painfully at the roots of our moral malaise. The movie sees us clear, the way we were, everywhere."

Richard Cuskelly in the *Los Angeles Herald Examiner:*
"It is the first unblinking, unblushing, unembarrassed sorting of the social confusions in which we all found ourselves floundering in the late 1960s . . . *Shampoo,* as blunt as any major Hollywood film has yet dared to be, will provoke shocked gasps and shrieks of laughter for its abundance of outrageous one-liners."

Goldie Hawn waxes pensive amidst beddy-bye doings with Beatty.

Hawn and Beatty hold a confab at the beauty parlor.

Lee Grant gives Beatty the business.

*Lee Grant, Jack Warden, Julie Christie and
Beatty find things getting tense.*

The Fortune

CAST:
Warren Beatty *(Nicky)*; Jack Nicholson *(Oscar)*; Stockard Channing *(Freddie)*; Florence Stanley *(Landlady)*; Richard B. Shull *(Chief Detective)*; Tom Newman *(John the Barber)*; John Fiedler *(Police Photographer)*; Scatman Crothers *(Fisherman)*; Dub Taylor *(Rattlesnake Tom)*; Ian Wolfe *(Justice of the Peace)*; Rose Michtom *(His Wife)*; Brian Avery *(Airline Steward)*; Nira Barab *(Girl Lover)*; Christopher Guest *(Boy Lover)*; Jim Antonio *(First Policeman)*; Vic Vallaro *(Second Policeman)*; Joe Tornatore *(Detective)*; Kathryn Grody *(Police Secretary)*; George Roberts *(Officer)*.

Beatty in his 1920s makeup

The boys have a heart-to-heart.

CREDITS:
Mike Nichols and Don Devlin *(Producers);* Hank Moonjean *(Executive Producer);* Mike Nichols *(Director);* Adrien Joyce *(Writer);* John A. Alonza, A.S.C. *(Director of Photography);* David Shire *(Music Adaptor and Conductor);* Richard Sylbert *(Production Designer);* Robert E. Schultz *(Associate Producer);* Stu Linder *(Film Editor);* W. Stewart Campbell *(Art Director);* George Gaines *(Set Decorator);* Arthur R. Schmidt *(Assistant Editor);* Bertil G. Hallberg *(Sound Mixer);* Dick Vorisek *(Re-recording Mixer);* Howard Roessel *(Unit Production Manager);* Peter Bogart *(Assistant Director);* Jerry Grandey *(Second Assistant Director);* Richard Liebegott *(Production Coordinator);* Annabel Davis-Goff *(Script Supervisor.)* The background music includes: "I Must Be Dreaming" (Al Dubin, Pat Flaherty and Al Sherman);

"Pretty Trix" (Joe Venuti and Eddie Lang); "My Honey's Lovin' Arms" (Joseph Meyer and Herman Ruby); "Shaking the Blues Away" (Irving Berlin); "Cigarette Tango" (John H. Densmore); "You've Got to See Mama Every Night or You Can't See Mama at All" (Billy Rose and Con Conrad).

Opened at the Coronet Theatre, New York, May 20, 1975. Running time, 88 minutes.

In his second 1975 film, *The Fortune,* Beatty was outplayed by Jack Nicholson, an actor with far greater native talent and a relaxed, easy spontaneity in his playing. Mike Nichols, of *The Graduate* fame, directed this film which attempted to blend, not too successfully, farce and camp nostalgia.

Walking on the beach — two guys with a secret

Beatty photographed after the "murder" breaks

Beatty gives the cops an argument.

Jack Nicholson had brought the script to Nichols originally, stating that he thought it had great possibilities for an amusing period farce. Unfortunately the Adrien Joyce original script looked better on paper than it came to look on film. It did boast an enchanting new actress, Stockard Channing, who ran rings around Beatty and gave Nicholson a run for his honors.

In describing his directorial method during shooting, Nichols said: "I worked with the actors. We all did it together. We rehearsed on the basis of trying to figure out what the scene is about, what are the secrets in it? I hope the film is a light comedy, but the secret is the caricature of how people treat each other and it is taken to an insane length."

Rather than attempt to shoot 1920s-style scenes on current Los Angeles locations, with their TV antennas and compact cars, a replica of a 1920s Los Angeles street was constructed on the studio lot. And Nichols and his researchers tried faithfully to get the feel of the period. "In the '20s," Nichols said, "news clippings were about love nests, famous murders. There was a grand feeling in the country that you could do anything you wanted to do, like learn to play the piano by mail, a feeling and mood in the whole country. I tried to get it on film. There were famous murders, famous heiresses."

Beatty put on a Ramon Novarro moustache and slicked down his hair. And Nicholson submitted to curlers, resulting in a frizzy-haired look that changed his image if hardly his on-screen persona. *"That,"* Nicholson has laughed, "is irreplaceable, unchangeable, irredeemable."

The critics received it coolly for the most part, though a lot of publicity hoopla indigenous to the mid-70s tried to disguise its limitations and to some extent succeeded. Typical review was that of *Time,* which said, *"The Fortune* is a bleak, frostbitten farce, desperate for invention and rather a sham." The hour-and-a-half film (short-subject length in these days of mammoth movies) has Beatty, a cad, and Nicholson, an embezzler, rooking heiress Channing into a false elopement, with the Nicholson character marrying her though she plans to bed down with Beatty, who unfortunately is legally married to someone else. To avoid running afoul of the Mann Act, they employ the marriage gimmick. Of course the two mountebanks are after the heiress's money (her dad made a fortune in sanitary napkins, and this is made the subject of a lame, tasteless anecdote by Nicholson concerning his mother's sending

him to the store to buy "mouse-beds"—a term she used to protect his youthful innocence).

Of course Nicholson lusts after their female prey and finds a way to make her his wife in actuality as well as in name. There is a lot of comic scuffling, one-upmanship and whatnot between Beatty and Nicholson. When the heiress discovers their mercenary motives, she threatens to give her money to charity, and then the boys come up with a murder plan—they will set her afloat in a trunk. But the trunk doesn't settle, she comes back to the motel, Nicholson panics meanwhile and blabs out to the cops a confession to a murder that in actuality was never committed, the girl realizes what nefarious chaps she has taken up with but decides to stay with them anyway, and, well, you have the idea.

Nicholson comes off best in the picture, though there is a slyness underlying his buffoonery that makes it hard to accept his comic bungling beyond a point. However, in comic skills, personality force, and natural ease, he far outpoints

Beatty has problems with landlady Florence Stanley.

Beatty, who seems strained, ill-at-ease, tense, and obviously anxious, in more than one scene, for director Nichols to yell "Cut and print!"

More than one critic remarked on the lack of genuine wit and style, the strained, forced "comic" situations. Every ancient sight gag and vintage laugh-milker is dragged in by the ear: snoopy landlady gags, the bit about not being able to slip wedding rings onto fingers without much to-do, Channing's less-than-competent cooking skills, etc. A sophomoric attempt to drown the heiress in a shallow birdbath is labored to a fare-thee-well. All in all, *The Fortune* did not fare so well with the critics. Better, though, with the public, who were taken in by shrewd publicity and the star-power combine of Beatty and Nicholson.

REVIEWS:
Paul D. Zimmerman in *Newsweek:*
"There is something hectic and ugly about watching a cad and a weasel trying to drown, however ineptly, an essentially defenseless innocent. *Fortune's* balance is cockeyed, and the romantic-comedy genre itself, designed for light-hearted larking, is too thin to contain such an ultimately heartless vision of human relationships, capped by Channing's incomprehensible return to her malefactors' arms at the finish. One is left longing for Mike Nichols, the brilliant satirist who made us laugh at our foibles, but who seems to have given way to a cynical, grimly grinning moralist . . . he creates a comic *Chinatown,* a moral wasteland of mean motives and faithless acts in which comedy cannot flourish."

Marsha McCreadie in *Films in Review:*
"*The Fortune* is full of delightful turnarounds. Director Mike Nichols gives us a new Jack Nicholson . . . the 'brains' of the outfit is Warren Beatty, effectively pompous and stiff . . . Not all the bits work and the rhythm goes awry at times (though perhaps Nichols wishes to disturb our perspective). But the dialogue is wittily tongue-in-cheek

With the sinister trunk on the shore

Two profiles of what well-dressed 1920s men wear

. . . and there's an unerring eye for the period-piece squalors of Southern California bungalow life and for the popular fantasies that pervade and motivate us all, no matter when we live."

"Murf." in *Variety:*
"A silly, shallow, occasionally enjoyable comedy trifle . . . very classy 1920s production values often merit more attention than the plot . . . like many a vintage Warner Bros. film, the comedy emerges from shrill shouting matches between the principals. Nicholson works harder, and is more effective than Beatty, who seems cold and stiff throughout. Channing has the advantage of a showpiece part—the type that first brought Madeline Kahn to attention."

Jerry Oster in *The New York Daily News:*
"An animated *Bartlett's Familiar Quotations* of those recent movies about the '20s and '30s, an expensive redundancy, a painful illustration of the limitations of the star system, [the film] is notable only in that it is quite possibly the last picture of its kind . . . cast for their box-office clout, without consideration of whether they're really a good team, Warren Beatty as Nicky, and Jack Nicholson as Oscar, get all knotted up in their idiosyncrasies. Each is a subtle scene-stealer, and the intensity with which they work at it keeps them from playing off each other with anything like the effectiveness that Paul Newman and Robert Redford had in *The Sting.* . . . I like the way Nichols directs. I like his long takes

205

Stockard Channing gets the once-over from an admirer.

and use of the depth of the frame and the way he takes the camera to the action, minimizing the need for cuts and achieving a nice grace and fluidity. But it's a demanding style, and especially for Beatty, who's always so tense, one that is too strict for comedy. At times, Beatty looks as if he'll pop if Nichols doesn't yell 'cut!' "

Vincent Canby in *The New York Times:*
"It's a marvelous attempt to recreate a kind of farce that, with the notable exceptions of a handful of films by Blake Edwards and Billy Wilder, disappeared after World War II. . . . Mr. Beatty's

role is less flamboyant than Mr. Nicholson's but he plays straight with determined comedy style. . . . though it's only ninety-five minutes long, which is virtually a short subject these days, [the film] does have sequences that sag, and there are moments when it's obvious that farce is not exactly the native art of any of the people involved. One is occasionally aware of the tremendous effort that has gone into a particular effect . . . the endeavor is nobly conceived in an era that has just about abandoned farce in favor of parody, satire, situation and/or wisecrack comedy."

Channing and Beatty talk while Nicholson pulls up his underwear in rear.

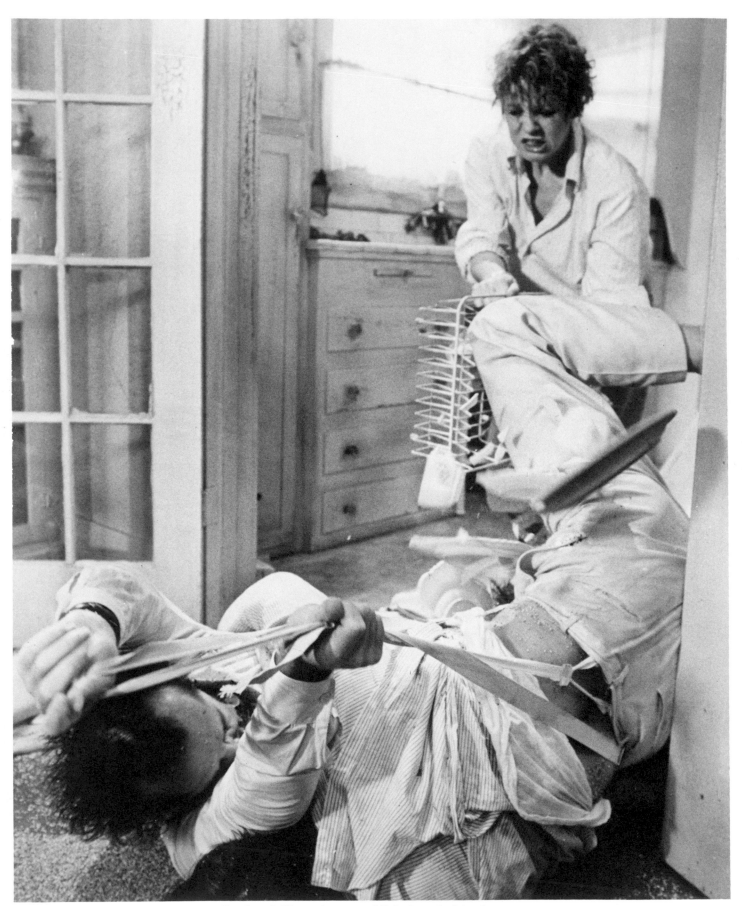

Stockard Channing puts Nicholson in his place.

Nicholson and Beatty with official escorts

Heaven Can Wait

CAST:

Warren Beatty *(Joe Pendleton);* Julie Christie *(Betty Logan);* James Mason *(Mr. Jordan);* Jack Warden *(Max Corkle);* Charles Grodin *(Tony Abbott);* Dyan Cannon *(Julia Farnsworth);* Buck Henry *(The Escort);* Vincent Gardenia *(Det. Krim);* Joseph Maher *(Sisk);* Dolph Sweet *(Head Coach);* R.G. Armstrong *(Team Manager);* John Randolph *(Former Team Owner);* William Sylves-

Warren Beatty

The famous athletic-togs-and-wings ad

ter *(Nuclear Reporter)*; Keene Curtis *(Oppenheim)*; Hamilton Camp *(Bentley)*; Jeannie Linero *(Lavinia)*; Arthur Malet *(Everett)*; Stephanie Faracy *(Corinne)*.

CREDITS:
Warren Beatty *(Producer and Director)*; Buck Henry *(Co-Director)*; Howard W. Koch Jr. and Charles H. Maguire *(Executive Producers)*; Warren Beatty and Elaine May *(Screenwriters)*; Based on the play by Harry Segall; William A. Fraker *(Director of Photography)*; Movielab Color; Robert C. Jones and Don Zimmerman *(Editors)*; Dave Grusin *(Music)*; Paul Sylbert *(Production Design)*; Edwin O'Donovan *(Art Direction)*; George Gaines *(Set Decoration)*; John K. Wilkinson, Tommy Overton *(Sound)*; Theodora Van Runkle, Richard Bruno, Mike Hoffman, Arlene Encell *(Costumes-Wardrobe)*.

Opened at Loew's Tower East, Loew's State 2 and Showcase Theatres, New York, June 28, 1978. Running time, 101 minutes.

After a three-year absence from the screen, Beatty reappeared with an elegant, slickly-tooled remake of Robert Montgomery's 1941 hit, *Here Comes Mr. Jordan*. He retitled the film *Heaven Can Wait*. (This was the title of Harry Segall's Broadway play from which the first film was adapted. A Don Ameche–Gene Tierney 1943 film usurped the title for a film with a different plot.)

Released in June 1978, this handsomely mounted, tasteful film has so far made upwards of $60,000,000 — a tribute to Beatty's well-conceived and executed merchandising and promotional techniques, which he had also employed to prime advantage with *Bonnie and Clyde* and *Shampoo*. The film played its initial runs through

211

Warren Beatty

James Mason lays down the law to Beatty.

the summer of 1978, thus taking advantage of the June-September vacation film attendance boom. The film caught on all over the country, and garnered a set of reviews that were, in the main, favorable.

Some commentators thought *Heaven Can Wait* Beatty's answer to Katharine Hepburn's earlier public complaint that he was not making affirmative, inspiring and upbeat films. Certainly this was an inoffensive item, amounting to wholesome entertainment that, while old-fashioned in concept, still managed to be brightly amusing, and was deftly written and acted.

The 1941 original, released by Columbia and directed by Alexander Hall, displayed Montgomery as a prizefighter who dies before his time has come, and who is sent back to earth, where he discovers that his body has been cremated. Mr. Jordan (Claude Rains), the Heavenly Mr. Fix-It, helps Montgomery look around for another body in which to spend the decades on earth yet left to him. Metaphysical and romantic complications abound after Montgomery gets his new body.

In Beatty's and Elaine May's reworking of the theme (Beatty also produced and co-directed, with Buck Henry), the prizefighter becomes an aging star quarterback for the Los Angeles Rams. James Mason, in the Rains part, helps Beatty find another body after Buck Henry, a goof-off "escort," has dragged Beatty heavenward before his time after a freak auto accident in a tunnel. Beatty winds up in the body of an industrial tycoon, one Farnsworth, whose wife, Dyan Cannon, and secretary, Charles Grodin, are plotting his

213

Beatty befuddled by his strange fate

murder. Beatty proceeds to flounder and fuss around as he tries to get on top of the affairs of his new character, while coping with the complaints, and later romantic addressals, of a militant Englishwoman (Julie Christie) who demands that the industrialist's company give up plans to supersede her village with a mammoth refinery. Beatty tries to resume his football career in his new body, but events force him to return yet again to the celestial world where yet another body is chosen for him. Then comes the problem of making Miss Christie understand that the spirit of the man she loves is in the new man; at the end it seems that she will "get it."

The Movielab color is excellent, the settings handsome, the tone elegant. There is much taste displayed in the production values, and the acting is topnotch. Mason, urbane and authoritative in his best style, makes a worthy successor to Rains as Mr. Jordan, Miss Christie is warm and winning in the role originally played by Evelyn Keyes, and Jack Warden, Charles Grodin and Dyan Cannon are all in top form in the roles essayed in 1941 by such as James Gleason, John

Emery and Rita Johnson. Grodin and Cannon add immeasurably to the picture's class and style with sharply humorous performances as the conniving wife and her lover, and make the most of the clever and amusing lines dreamed up by Elaine May, Beatty's co-writer. (What with co-writing, co-directing, producing, etc., this film, Beatty certainly put in a claim for the title of Hollywood's current "Renaissance Man.")

The rather sentimentalized supernatural aspects of the admittedly dated theme are handled with a light, fey, shrewdly sophisticated touch that never gets heavy or unduly intrusive, and while Beatty lacks Robert Montgomery's expert touch with this type of material, fragile and elusive as it is, he does offer a quietly ingratiating performance that is his best in years. Though forty-one when the picture was made, he displays a lithe, youthful joie-de-vivre both in manner and appearance — a tribute to his disciplined physical conditioning.

There is nothing monumental about *Heaven Can Wait*, but it is a testimonial to the good intentions of all who made it, and in its unassuming

Telling the announcer all about the game

Communing with Julie Christie

Buck Henry (right) is reproached by Mason and Beatty for his goof.

Beatty gets Christie into a thoughtful mood.

way it clicks. It also highlights, in concrete form, Beatty's commendable desire to make tasteful fare for today's audiences that makes up in wit and style for the fantastic, gossamer elements which, even in 1941, seemed riskily far-out.

REVIEWS:
"Murf." in *Variety:*
"The years have been good to Beatty in that there is now a bedrock of maturity in his screen charisma without any loss of the quiet exuberance that has endured. . . . Script and direction are very strong, providing a rich mix of visual and verbal humor that is controlled and avoids the

extremes of cheap vulgarity and overly esoteric whimsy . . . the entire cast is excellent."

Vincent Canby in *The New York Times:*
"[The film] gives the impression of being a swinging 1978 romantic comedy struggling to free itself from the body of the 1941 film. Most of the time it remains locked in, embraced by the unyielding requirements of its elaborate, facetious plot gimmick. . . . . The surprise is that *Heaven Can Wait* is as much fun as it is when it has to waste so much energy in the service of a gimmick that we would now endure only in a pilot film for a projected television series titled *I Dream of*

*The souls wait their turn for transference to the
Other World (Beatty and Buck Henry in left background).*

Beatty and Julie Christie reach an understanding.

Beatty gets ready for the Big Game.

Joey. [The film] is a hybrid of no great style but of a good deal of charm and with a marvelous cast. . . . it has a kind of earnest cheerfulness that is sometimes most winning. Mr. Beatty and Miss Christie are performers who bring to their roles the easy sort of gravity that establishes characters of import, no matter how simply they are drawn in the script."

Rex Reed in *The New York Daily News:*
"At a demoralizing time in movie history when trash like *Jaws 2* and *Grease* still sucks in the suckers, *Heaven Can Wait* is all the more winning because it doesn't leave you heavy-hearted, depressed or frightened out of your wits; it lifts the spirits and makes you feel good about life on earth and even beyond. If the angels are as witty and human as they are in this joyous film, Heaven just might be worth waiting for."

Archer Winsten in the *New York Post:*
"The amalgam of heavenly mysticism, vile commercial murder, serious pro football and comic miscues makes *Heaven Can Wait* an entertainment of neatly carpentered surprises. [But] it's a picture in which the sum of excellent parts does not add up to an exhilarating total. It's not quite a sequel, but the basic design is not fresh, and the new patches are serviceable without becoming works of art in themselves."

Molly Haskell in *New York* magazine:
"The fantasy of two lovers transcending time and their own physical bodies is a fragile one, and even in the forties it hung by a gossamer thread. It was sustained by the make-believe studio world of black-and-white photography—a far cry from the robustly colored, here-and-now world of Super Bowls and Southern California where Beatty's version is set. The poster ad showing a winged Beatty is a double tease, as we know he could neither die nor become an angel. His ultraphysical presence dominates the film, an ego trip in which Death, like everyone else, is on the Beatty payroll. . . . It is not the character he plays but the disingenuousness with which he plays it that gives Beatty's performance its fascination. As a sex idol, Beatty is too calculating to have the direct appeal of the old stars (as a fantasy lover, you'd want to kiss him—if you wanted to at all— only with your eyes open). But watching him apply the hard and soft arts of self-merchandising is a dazzling spectacle in its own right."